# Buckle Down®

## to the
## Common Core
## State Standards

## English Language Arts

## Grade 3

CENTRAL ELEMENTARY SCHOOL

This book belongs to: _____

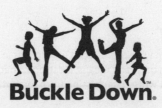

**Buckle Down®**

*Helping your schoolhouse meet the standards of the statehouse™*

## Acknowledgment

Every effort has been made by the publisher to locate each owner of the copyrighted material reprinted in this publication and to secure the necessary permissions. If there are any questions regarding the use of these materials, the publisher will take appropriate corrective measures to acknowledge ownership in future publications.

ISBN 978-0-7836-8049-1

1CCUS03RD01

7 8 9 10

Cover Image: Winding road through the forest in the Appalachian Mountains.
© Alexey Stiop/Dreamstime.com

**Triumph Learning®** 136 Madison Avenue, 7th Floor, New York, NY 10016

© 2011 Triumph Learning, LLC

Buckle Down is an imprint of Triumph Learning®

# Frequently Asked Questions about the Common Core State Standards

**What are the Common Core Standards?**

The Common Core Standards for English Language Arts, grades K–12, are a set of shared goals and expectations for what knowledge and skills will help students succeed. They allow students to understand what is expected of them and to become progressively more proficient in understanding and using English Language Arts. At the same time, teachers will be better equipped to know exactly what they need to help students learn and establish individualized benchmarks for them.

**Will the Common Core Standards tell teachers how and what to teach?**

No. The best understanding of what works in the classroom comes from the teachers who are in them. That's why these standards will establish *what* students need to learn, but they will not dictate *how* teachers should teach. Instead, schools and teachers will decide how best to help students reach the standards.

**What will the Common Core Standards mean for students?**

The standards will provide more clarity about and consistency in what is expected of student learning across the country. Common standards will not prevent different levels of achievement among students, but they will ensure more consistent exposure to materials and learning experiences through curriculum, instruction, and teacher preparation among other supports for student learning. These standards will help prepare students with the knowledge and skills they need to succeed in college and careers.

**Do the Common Core Standards focus on skills and content knowledge?**

Yes. The Common Core Standards recognize that both content and skills are important. The Common Core Standards contain rigorous content and application of knowledge through high-order thinking skills. The English Language Arts standards require certain critical content for all students, including: classic myths and stories from around the world, America's founding documents, foundational American literature, and Shakespeare. The remaining crucial decisions about what content should be taught are left to state and local determination. In addition to content coverage, the Common Core State Standards require that students systematically acquire knowledge in literature and other disciplines through reading, writing, speaking, and listening.

The Common Core Standards also require that students develop a depth of understanding and ability to apply English Language Arts to novel situations, as college students and employees regularly do.

**Will common assessments be developed? When will they be ready?**

It will be up to the states: some states plan to come together voluntarily to develop a common assessment system. A state-led consortium on assessment would be grounded in the following principles: allow for comparison across students, schools, districts, states, and nations; create economies of scale; provide information and support more effective teaching and learning; and prepare students for college and careers.

A common assessment could be in place in some states by the 2014–2015 school year.

# TABLE OF CONTENTS

### To the Teacher:

Common Core Standards are listed for each lesson in the table of contents and for each page in the shaded gray bars that run across the tops of the pages in the workbook (see the example at right).

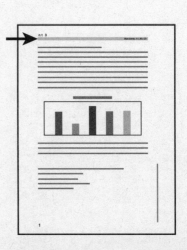

# UNIT 1

# Reading

Before you could read, letters probably looked like a secret code. Later, you learned that code when you found out that each letter makes it own sound (or sounds). As you put those sounds together, you made words. Then, you put those words together into sentences and full stories and books.

In this unit, you'll learn how to gather information to understand what you read. As you read, you can use many different tools to learn the meaning of new words. These tools will help you understand passages, stories, and books. If you practice using these tools, you will become a better reader.

7

# Lesson 1: Learning New Words

Did you know there are hundreds of thousands of words in the English language? This means that even grown-ups sometimes see words they don't know.

You may even *confront* (meet) a word that is *alien* (strange) to you in a comic book. Don't *fret* (worry)!

When you see a new word, don't give up. Be a detective, just like Sherlock Holmes. Look for clues to help you figure out the word. Usually, you will be able to find these clues in the reading passage. You just have to know what to look for. This lesson will show you how to become a word detective.

 **TIP 1: Start by sounding out an unknown word.**

If you don't know a word by sight, the first thing to do is to sound it out. Let's imagine that you read the following sentence in a story:

Melina loves to fly her kite in the park when there is a strong <u>wind</u>.

*Wind* has more than one meaning. You're not sure which meaning is used. So, you sound it out. It could rhyme with *kind* and mean "to wrap around, turn, or curve." Or it could rhyme with *pinned* and mean "blowing air." Which way sounds correct?

1. As it is used in this sentence, what should the word *wind* rhyme with?

_____

**TIP 2: Sound out the word until you recognize it.**

There are many words in the English language, and some are spelled in unusual and irregular ways. Even if a word is irregularly spelled, sound it out until you recognize it.

The following are some irregularly spelled words you may already know:

| Word | How to Pronounce the Word | Meaning |
|---|---|---|
| *although* | awl-thoh | in spite of, even though |
| *machine* | muh-sheen | a structure that completes a task |
| *science* | seye-ens | the study of the universe |
| *stomach* | stuhm-uhk | a part inside the body that digests food |

 **Practice Activity 1**

**Directions:** Read the following irregularly spelled words. Sound out each word. Then, write the meaning of the word, and write the word in a sentence. The first one has been done for you.

1. heart

   <u>The word *heart* means a part of the body that pumps blood or a part of the body that loves. My grandmother is sweet and has a big heart.</u>

2. friend

   _____

   _____

3. stomach

   _____

   _____

CCSs: RF.3.3d, RL.3.10, L.3.4a

As you read this story about Sherlock Holmes, think about how you might figure out what the unknown or irregularly spelled words mean.

# *Sherlock Holmes and the Case of the Wheediddle*
## by Sandi Shaw

*Sherlock Holmes put his violin back in its case. He stared once again at the note that had been slipped under his door. It was very, very strange. The writer had used many words that Sherlock and his partner, Dr. Watson, did not know. Holmes would have to look for clues to understand the note.*

Daab Mr. Holmes,

     Can we meet at 8 o'grock? Wait for me. I hope I'm not lorgh. Sometimes I forget to put a new battery in my wheediddle and it stops. Then I don't know what time it is. I'll meet you at the bongle of Baker Street and 10th Avenue. Try not to be lorgh!

                      Very truly yongs,
                      Hobart Tinwhistle

"Well," said Sherlock, "*Daab* must mean 'Dear' since most letters begin with that word. And *o'grock* could mean 'o'clock,' since it is matched with the number 8."

The great detective continued to study the letter. "*Wheediddle* must mean 'watch' or 'clock,' since the writer says that his wheediddle stops when he doesn't put a new battery in it—and then he doesn't know what time it is.

"*Lorgh* must mean 'late.' He hopes he won't be late if his watch stops. Then, later in the note, he tells me not to be 'lorgh.' Yes, I am certain that *lorgh* means 'late,'" Sherlock said to himself. "*Bongle* must mean 'corner,' since Baker Street crosses 10th Avenue.

"And, finally," the detective said, "*yongs* must mean 'yours.' Mr. Tinwhistle is probably trying to close his letter with 'Very truly yours.'

"Dr. Watson!" Sherlock called excitedly. "Come. Grab your coat and hat. We must meet a certain Mr. Tinwhistle at the corner of Baker Street and 10th Avenue at 8 o'clock. And," he added, "we must not be 'lorgh'!"

CCSs: L.3.4a, RF.3.4c

 **TIP 3: Don't stop reading when you come to a word you don't know.**

Here's the best way to understand a new word. Use other words you already know to help you! Don't stop reading just because you don't know a word. Say it to yourself, and then go right on reading.

Sometimes, other words in the passage will give context clues to the meaning of the new word. These words often are found close together. Sometimes they are even in the same sentence. Look at these examples:

- In this area, we can find <u>gabbro</u>, a type of dark, heavy rock.

- She looked in her coin purse and found one <u>dinar</u>.

- Tom <u>assures</u> his good health by running and eating healthy foods.

2. What is *gabbro*?

   _____

3. What is a *dinar*?

   _____

4. What is the meaning of *assures*?

   _____

Sometimes reading the whole paragraph will help you figure out the meaning of an unknown word. Read the following paragraph. It tells about an imaginary thing called a *gorfle*. Try to figure out what a *gorfle* is.

> <u>Gorfles</u> are beautiful and very useful. A full-grown gorfle is big enough to make shade in the summer. In the spring, its blossoms have a wonderful smell. A gorfle has strong branches that hold a lot of juicy fruit.

5. What do you know about a *gorfle* from reading the paragraph?

   _____

   _____

6. Based on the paragraph, what is a *gorfle*?

   A. a kind of tree

   B. a kind of vegetable

   C. a kind of flower

   D. a kind of weed

7. Look back at Mr. Tinwhistle's letter on page 10. Underline details that give clues to the meaning of *wheediddle*.

 **TIP 4: Go back to the passage and put your finger on the unknown word.**

A question on a reading test might ask you the meaning of a word or phrase. A **phrase** is a group of words. First, find the word or phrase in the passage. Then use the words around it to figure out its meaning. Keep your finger on the word so you don't lose your place when you look back at the question.

CCSs: L.3.4a, RF.3.4c

 **TIP 5:** **Try each multiple-choice answer in place of the unknown word.**

When you are asked the meaning of a word, find the word in the passage. Replace the unknown word with each answer choice, one at a time. The answer that makes the most sense is probably correct.

Read the following paragraph.

> I think most people called him Charlie Cheeseburger. But that was a long time ago. To the best of my <u>recollection</u>, he never called himself by that name. In fact, he hated cheeseburgers. And his real name was Albert.

Read the following question, but don't answer it yet.

8. What is the meaning of the word *recollection*?

   A. eyesight
   B. memory
   C. touch
   D. smell

First, find the sentence that contains the word *recollection*. Then try each answer choice in place of the word *recollection*. Which answer choice makes the most sense in the sentence?

Now go back and answer Number 8.

 **TIP 6:** **Check the passage for words with the same meaning.**

If you read a word that you don't know, you will probably find all sorts of clues to the word's meaning in the passage.

Sometimes, the passage will have other words with nearly the same meaning as the word you are trying to figure out.

Read the following passage, and then answer Numbers 9 and 10.

> The old man was very poor. Each day he would labor in his field until he was so tired that he could barely move. As the sun set, the old man would stop his hard work. Then he would throw his hoe over his shoulder and slowly walk home to his small cottage.

9. Circle any words or phrases in the passage that you think might be close to the same meaning as the word *labor*.

10. Which word means about the same thing as the word *labor*?

   A. work

   B. laugh

   C. daydream

   D. wander

 **TIP 7: Check the passage for words with opposite meanings.**

Sometimes the passage will give you clues to the opposite meaning of a word. If you can figure out a word's opposite, you can make a good guess about its meaning.

Read the following sentences. Then answer Numbers 11 and 12.

> Carmen was usually very prompt for her music lesson. However, today she was 10 minutes late.

11. Circle any words in the sentences that you think might have the opposite meaning of *prompt*.

12. Which word means the opposite of the word *prompt*?

   A. sad

   B. late

   C. unhappy

   D. puzzled

CCSs: RI.3.4, L.3.6

 **TIP 8: Use clues to understand academic words.**

**Academic words** are words you use in specific classes at school. Sometimes you'll find these words in your textbooks. Examples of academic words are *character*, *hypothesis*, *summary*, and others. Often details in a text give you clues about the meanings of academic words.

The following are some academic words you may already know:

| Word | Meaning | Example |
|---|---|---|
| *cell* | basic unit of all living things | The plant cell has a strong cell wall. |
| *character* | a person represented in fiction | The main character likes dogs. |
| *fiction* | a type of writing that contains made-up details: a short story, a novel, a play, or a poem | The story about talking rabbits is fiction. |
| *nonfiction* | a type of writing that is made up of facts | This encyclopedia is nonfiction. |
| *geography* | the study of Earth's surface and weather | The geography of the United States made it hard for people to travel West. |
| *government* | a system that rules a community | The government is democratic. |
| *hypothesis* | a guess that can be tested | The experiment tested our hypothesis. |
| *summary* | a brief statement of important facts or details | I wrote a summary of the book. |
| *timeline* | a drawing that shows the dates things happened | The timeline showed that the Civil War started in 1861. |
| *vote* | a way to share an opinion, a formal part of some governments | Yesterday was the day to vote! |

**Practice Activity 2**

**Directions:** Read the following paragraph.

For homework, I wrote a short story about a character named Joy. My teacher told me to include a lot of <u>details</u>, so I described Joy's laugh, her friends, and what she likes to do.

Read the following question, but don't answer it yet.

1. What is the meaning of the word *detail*?

    A. a sentence

    B. a dictionary

    C. a description

    D. a generalization

First, look in the paragraph for clues about the meaning of the word *detail*. Then, define the word *detail* in your own words.

Now go back and answer Number 1.

CCS: L.3.4d

 **TIP 9:** **Use a dictionary to find out what words mean.**

A **dictionary** is a book that lists words and their definitions. It tells what words mean and how to say them.

A dictionary can help you figure out the meaning of key words and phrases in a reading passage. First, see how the word is spelled in the passage. Then, find that word in the dictionary. Remember, words in a dictionary are in ABC order.

Let's say you have found the word *stick* in a passage. Here is what the dictionary tells you about the word *stick*.

---

### stick – stink    180

| | | | | | | |
|---|---|---|---|---|---|---|
| **a** | bat | **i** | sit | **oi** | boil | **a** in alike |
| **ā** | able | **ī** | iron | **ou** | our | **e** in shaken |
| **ä** | car | **o** | not | **u** | nut | **i** in beautiful |
| **e** | set | **ō** | over | **u̇** | put | **o** in bacon |
| **ē** | easy | **ô** | cord | **ü** | ruler | **u** in circus |
| **ėr** | germ | | | | | |

ə = { **a** in alike, **e** in shaken, **i** in beautiful, **o** in bacon, **u** in circus }

**stick¹** (stik) *noun* **1:** a woody piece or part of a tree or bush: as **(a)** a twig or thin branch **(b)** a cut or broken branch or piece of wood **2 a:** a long, thin piece of wood: as (1): a club or pole used as a weapon (2): a walking stick, cane **b:** a tool used for hitting an object in a game **3:** any tools that look like a stick: as **(a)** an airplane lever that operates wing controls **(b)** the gear lever on a car **4:** a piece of furniture **5:** a long, thin piece (*stick* of butter, *stick* of candy)

**stick²** (stik) *verb* **1:** poke with a pointed tool **2:** put into a position (*stick* it in the closet) **3:** attach to **4:** stay near (*my puppy sticks to my heels*) **5:** stretch out of (*stick your head out and check for rain*)

---

**17**

**Practice Activity 3**

**Directions:** Read each sentence. Then choose the correct meaning of the word *stick* or *sticks* by using the dictionary entry on page 17.

1. The birds built their nest out of small <u>sticks</u>.

   A. twigs

   B. canes

   C. clubs

   D. levers

2. Nicole told her little sister, "<u>Stick</u> with me while we cross the street."

   A. poke with a needle

   B. stay near

   C. put into a position

   D. attach to

3. William gave me a <u>stick</u> of gum.

   A. broken branch

   B. twig

   C. long, thin piece

   D. tool in a game

4. The player took his hockey <u>stick</u> and hit the puck across the ice.

   A. piece of furniture

   B. tool used in a game

   C. cut or broken branch

   D. a type of ruler

5. The man moved with the help of a walking <u>stick</u>.

   A. cane

   B. tool

   C. lever

   D. twig

**TIP 10: Use a glossary to look up the meanings of words.**

Some books have a glossary. A **glossary** is like a dictionary of every important word in a book. The glossary lists words in ABC order. It is found near the back of a book.

Look at this glossary from a science book. Then answer Number 13.

---

**Glossary**

**A**

**accurate:** as exact as possible

**B**

**balanced diet:** a diet that gives your body everything it needs to stay healthy and to grow

**basic needs:** things that all living creatures must have in order to live: food, water, clean air, and shelter

**biologist:** a scientist who studies living things

**C**

**claim:** a statement someone wants others to believe is true

---

13. Which word has the closest meaning to *accurate*?

    A. exact
    B. healthy
    C. scientist
    D. statement

**Lesson Practice begins on the following page.**

**Directions:** This passage is about a boy who has to carry a birthday cake. Read the passage. Then answer Numbers 1 through 5.

# *Thinking Ahead*

by Wanda Wilson

Tony's aunt had promised. She said she'd give Tony five dollars. All he had to do was carry the birthday cake to the party down the street without ruining it.

"The deal is off if you drop it, kid," she said.

Tony walked along, holding the cake plate on either side with both hands. He was very careful not to trip on the sidewalk.

As he walked along, his <u>imagination</u> started to take over.

He thought to himself, *Once I <u>deliver</u> this cake, I will earn five dollars. With my aunt's five dollars, I will buy a bunch of lemonade mix. I'll start a lemonade stand. Then I can sell lemonade and make a whole lot of money. Then, I'll take that lemonade money and go shopping. I'll get a basketball <u>signed</u> by Nate Robinson. He's my favorite player of all time! My friends will all be <u>jealous</u>. They will want to play with the basketball. They will say, "Tony, c'mon, let me shoot!" But I won't let them. I will turn to face the basket and do a jump shot, like this!*

Tony's aunt asked him to carry the birthday cake.

Tony jumped. Forgetting all about the cake, he tossed it as if he were shooting a basket. The cake hit a tree, and globs of frosting and white cake flew everywhere. And just like that, all of Tony's basketball dreams vanished in a moment on 12th Avenue!

1. **Read this sentence from the story.**

   "As he walked along, his imagination started to take over."

   **The word *imagination* <u>most likely</u> means Tony**

   A. heard someone talking.

   B. pictured in his mind.

   C. remembered something.

   D. saw people walking by.

2. **The story says Tony is supposed to deliver the cake. What does the word *deliver* mean?**

   A. bring

   B. throw

   C. eat

   D. bake

3. **Read these sentences from the story.**

   "My friends will all be jealous. They will want to play with the basketball."

   **Which words from the sentences above help you know what *jealous* means?**

   A. "My friends"

   B. "will want"

   C. "play with"

   D. "the basketball"

4. **Read this sentence from the story.**

"I'll get a basketball signed by Nate Robinson."

**The word *signed* is an irregularly spelled word. What is the meaning of the word *signed*? What clues in the story show the meaning of the word *signed*?**

_____

_____

_____

# Lesson 2: Word Parts

As you learned in Lesson 1, you can use clues in a text to find the meanings of words. Sometimes you will need more help. The parts of a word can be useful helpers. This lesson tells you how to use parts of words to figure out the meanings of words.

## TIP 1: Separate words into sounds.

The English alphabet is made up of 26 letters. Each letter is either a vowel or a consonant. **Vowels** are the letters *a, e, i, o, u,* and sometimes *y.* **Consonants** are all the other letters.

Most words can be split up into parts using vowels and consonants. A **syllable** is a word part that makes its own sound. Syllables can be made up of a vowel or vowels with consonants.

Here are some examples of words broken into syllables:

climb / er          syl / la / ble

hos / pi / tal        wrin / kle

One easy way to count syllables is to put your hand just below your chin. Then say the word and count how many times your chin touches your hand. That is how many syllables the word has. Try it with the words you just read.

## Practice Activity 1

**Directions:** Circle the correct answers to Numbers 1 and 2.

1.  How many syllables does the word *chimpanzee* have?

    A. 1                         C. 3

    B. 2                         D. 4

2.  How many syllables does the word *supper* have?

    A. 1                         C. 3

    B. 2                         D. 4

**TIP 2:  Use root words and affixes to understand the meanings of words.**

Nonburnable / Non•burn•able

You may be thinking, *Oh, no! How can I ever learn to read words this long? Give me a break!*

That's exactly what the next tips will give you—several breaks. You'll learn how to break down a word into its parts.

The long word at the start of this section (*nonburnable*) is made up of three parts:

- The first part, *non-*, is a prefix. **Prefixes** are letters added to the beginning of a word.

- Next comes the root word, *burn*. A **root word** is a simple word. Groups of letters can be added to it to make new words.

- The last part of the word, *-able*, is a suffix. **Suffixes** are letters added to the end of a root word.

You can understand words with many parts by looking at their prefixes, roots, and suffixes. You can understand new words that have prefixes or suffixes added to known words.

Let's work through the example:

The root word *burn* is a known word. You already know that *burn* means "to set on fire."

Adding the prefix *non-* changes the meaning to "not burn."

Adding the suffix *-able* changes the meaning to "not able to be burned."

Let's take a closer look at these word parts. They may help you understand new words and what they mean.

 **TIP 3:  Remember your roots.**

Sometimes you can figure out what a word means by looking for the root. To do this, look for small words you know in the whole word. For example, the root word in *misspelled* is *spell*. The root word in *unfinished* is *finish*.

Here are some more root words for you to remember:

love       new       side       wind

CCSs: L.3.4b, L.3.4c, RF.3.3a

 **TIP 4: A prefix changes the meaning of a root word.**

A prefix is a set of letters added to the beginning of a root word. Adding a prefix changes the meaning of the root word.

Here's an example of a prefix at work:

$un$- + happy = unhappy
(prefix)   (root word)   (new word)

By adding *un-* to the root word *happy*, the meaning changes. It becomes the opposite. Instead of a good feeling (happy), we have a bad feeling (unhappy).

There are many prefixes in the English language. Here are some prefixes you should know:

| Prefix | Meaning | Example |
|---|---|---|
| | | (prefix + root word = new word) |
| *anti-* | against | *anti* + freeze = antifreeze |
| *bi-* | two | *bi* + cycle = bicycle |
| *co-* | together, with | *co* + operate = cooperate |
| *dis-* | not, away from | *dis* + agree = disagree |
| *ex-* | out, away from | *ex* + change = exchange |
| *fore-* | in front | *fore* + head = forehead |
| *im-* | not | *im* + patient = impatient |
| *in-* | not | *in* + complete = incomplete |
| *ir-* | not | *ir* + regular = irregular |
| *mid-* | middle | *mid* + night = midnight |
| *mis-* | wrong, poorly | *mis* + count = miscount |
| *non-* | not | *non* + sense = nonsense |
| *over-* | too much | *over* + due = overdue |
| *post-* | after | *post* + game = postgame |
| *pre-* | before | *pre* + heat = preheat |
| *re-* | again | *re* + paint = repaint |
| *un-* | not | *un* + comfortable = uncomfortable |

## Practice Activity 2

**Directions:** Read the following sentences. After each sentence, write a word with a prefix that has the same meaning as the underlined words. The first one has been done for you. You may use the list of prefixes on page 25 to help you.

1. Paul lost the race. He wanted to <u>run it again</u>.

   *rerun*

2. If you don't understand the story, <u>read it again</u>.

3. Shawna said that the story was <u>not true</u>.

4. Mother thought the babysitter was <u>paid too much</u>.

 ## Practice Activity 3

**Directions:** Read the following sentences. Write the meaning of the underlined word on the line that follows each sentence. The first one has been done for you. You may use the list of prefixes on page 25 to help you.

1. Justin's coach was <u>displeased</u> with his batting.

   *not pleased*

2. The airplane flew <u>nonstop</u> from Albany to Detroit.

3. Rose's tickets had been <u>prepaid</u>.

CCSs: L.3.4b, L.3.4c, RF.3.3a, RF.3.3b

 **TIP 5: Add letters to the end of a root word to make a suffix.**

Here's an example of a suffix at work:

enjoy + -*able* = enjoyable (able to be enjoyed)

The following are some suffixes you may already know:

| Suffix | Meaning | Example |
|---|---|---|
| | | (root word + suffix = new word) |
| -*able* | able to be | love + *able* = lovable |
| -*en* | having the nature of, | gold + *en* = golden |
| | to make or become | short + *en* = shorten |
| -*er* | one who does, | jump + *er* = jumper |
| | that which | boil + *er* = boiler |
| -*er* | more | fast + *er* = faster |
| -*est* | most | fast + *est* = fastest |
| -*ful* | full of | beauty + *ful* = beautiful |
| -*hood* | group of, | neighbor + *hood* = neighborhood |
| | state of | child + *hood* = childhood |
| -*ify* | to make, | beauty + *ify* = beautify |
| | to cause | |
| -*ion*/-*tion* | state of, | champ + *ion* = champion |
| | action of | collect + *ion* = collection |
| -*ity* | state of, | total + *ity* = totality |
| | condition | |
| -*less* | without | care + *less* = careless |
| -*ly* | in such a way | sad + *ly* = sadly |
| -*ment* | in a state of | excite + *ment* = excitement |
| -*sion*/-*tion* | an action | adopt + *ion* = adoption |
| -*sive*/-*tive* | tending to be | create + *ive* = creative |
| | a certain way | |
| -*sure*/-*ture* | a result or state of | mix + *ture* = mixture |

27

**Practice Activity 4**

**Directions:** Read the following sentences. After each sentence, write a word with a suffix that has the same meaning as the underlined words. The first one has been done for you. You may use the list of suffixes on page 27 to help you.

1. These clothes are <u>able to be washed</u>.

   *washable*
   _____

2. My bike helmet <u>tends to reflect</u> a lot of light.

   _____

3. Javier's father is <u>one who teaches</u>.

   _____

 **Practice Activity 5**

**Directions:** Read the following sentences. Write the meaning of the underlined word on the line that follows each sentence. The first one has been done for you. You may use the list of suffixes on page 27 to help you.

1. My kitten, Muffin, is very <u>lovable</u>.

   *able to be loved*
   _____

2. Marta used bleach to <u>whiten</u> her socks.

   _____

3. With a score of 113 to 6, winning the game seemed <u>hopeless</u>.

   _____

## Lesson Practice begins on the following page.

**Directions:** This passage is about two friends having fun in the summer. Read the passage. Then answer Numbers 1 through 3.

# *Our New Language*

Lynn lived in a full house with a lot of sisters and brothers! She hated how her sisters and brothers could always hear everything she said on the phone to her best friend Kayne. So she decided to come up with her own language.

"Belet's bego beto bethe bepark and beplay bebasketball," Lynn said into the phone in the kitchen. She stated it again just to make sure Kayne got it. Her sisters and brothers were unsure what Lynn was saying. There was clear confusion on their faces. "I'll be there in ten minutes," her friend Kayne said excitedly over the phone.

1. **How many syllables does the word *language* have?**

   A. 1          C. 3

   B. 2          D. 4

2. **Read this sentence from the story.**

   "She stated it again just to make sure Kayne understood."

   **Which of the following has the same meaning as the underlined words?**

   A. constated          C. unstated

   B. overstated          D. restated

3. **Read this sentence from the story.**

   "Her sisters and brothers were unsure what Lynn was saying."

   **What is the meaning of the underlined word?**

   A. not sure          C. able to be sure

   B. very sure          D. the state of being sure

CCSs: RL.3.10, RF.3.4a, RF.3.4b, RF.3.4c

# Lesson 3: Express Yourself!

Can you remember having a story read to you? The reader's voice might have changed during the story—getting soft during a tender moment or loud during an exciting moment. When you read aloud, you can express a lot about what you read using your voice. Think of yourself as an actor or actress! They use their voices to express feeling, information, and opinions. They pause at certain points so listeners can think about what they said. The way you speak tells your listeners a lot of information.

## TIP 1: Decide your purpose for reading.

You will know how to use your voice if you understand why you are reading a text. Are you reading for fun? Are you trying to solve a problem? There are many different reasons for reading. The following are some purposes you may already know:

| | | | |
|---|---|---|---|
| for fun | to learn something | to solve a problem | to take a test |
| to follow directions | to gather details | to make a decision | because you're curious |

When you are about to read aloud, think about your purpose. Ask yourself what you want to express to your listeners.

## Practice Activity 1

**Directions:** Read the following types of texts for Numbers 1 through 3. After each type of text, write your purpose for reading it aloud. You may use the list of purposes for reading to help you.

1. A dictionary entry that gives the meaning of a word

   _____

2. A poem about summertime

   _____

3. A bus schedule

   _____

CCSs: RF.3.4a, RF.3.4b

 **TIP 2: Change your voice as you read.**

There are clues in every text that tell you how to change your voice as you read. The punctuation in a text is a clue. **Punctuation** are the marks used to make meaning clear in a text. Examples of punctuation marks are the comma (,), period (.), question mark (?), exclamation point (!), and quotation marks (" ").

| Punctuation Mark | What It Expresses | What to Do While Reading |
| --- | --- | --- |
| *comma* (,) | a small idea, or a list of details | Pause for a brief moment, or take a quick breath. |
| *period* (.) | a stop at the end of a sentence | Pause for a moment, or take a full breath. |
| *question mark* (?) | a question | Make your voice go up higher. |
| *exclamation point* (!) | a command, a feeling of being surprised or angry | Express the right feeling: strength, shock, or anger. |
| *quotation marks* (" ") | words said aloud by a person or character | Say the words within the quotation marks the way the person or character would say them. |

**TIP 3: Know the best rate to use when reading aloud.**

You can choose the **rate**, or speed, you use to read different texts. Think about the type of text you are reading to decide the rate at which you should read.

Ask yourself these different questions:

- Are there a lot of common words or unusual words?

- If it is a story, is it a simple story and easy to understand? Or is it a complicated story and difficult to understand?

- If it is nonfiction, is the information easy to understand or is it difficult?

| When to read at a slower rate . . . | When to read at a faster rate . . . |
|---|---|
| If there are many unknown words | If there are many easy words |
| If there are many uncommon words | If there are many common words |
| If there are a lot of people or characters | If there are a few people or characters |
| If the story or information is complicated | If the story or information is simple |
| If there are a lot of important details | If there are only a few details |
| If there is a lot of new information | If there is a lot of common information |

 **TIP 4: Know when to change your rate when reading aloud.**

While you want to read at the best rate, you can also change your speed. When should you change your rate? You can change your rate when you think it will help you and your listeners.

The following are moments in a text when you should change your rate:

| What You Read | How to Change Your Rate |
|---|---|
| *If there are very important details* | Slow down to help readers hear all the information. |
| *If there is a sad moment* | Slow down to express the feelings. |
| *If there are directions* | Slow down to help readers understand the directions. |
| *If there is a lot of exciting action* | Speed up to express the action. |
| *If a character is excited* | Speed up to express the excitement. |

CCSs: RF.3.4b, RF.3.4c

 **TIP 5: Correct yourself by rereading the text aloud.**

Sometimes when you read aloud, you might **pronounce**, or say, a word incorrectly. You might read at a rate that you decide is wrong, or you might use your voice to express a feeling that you decide wasn't right for the text. These things happen to all readers! When they happen, you can go back and read aloud the text again correctly.

 **TIP 6: Using clues when reading aloud.**

Sometimes you will read aloud a word that you do not understand. Use clues in the text to help you read the word with the best voice, even though you may not know what the word means. You can also use clues in a text to figure out the meaning of the word.

Read aloud the following sentences. Each sentence includes a made-up word naming an imaginary thing. Use clues to read the unknown word the best way.

| Sentence | Clues | How to Read |
|---|---|---|
| Watch out for that scary <u>truffleunkus</u>! | The word "scary"<br><br>The exclamation point | Use your voice to express shock or fear when saying *truffleunkus*. |
| First step, put the <u>cranklekey</u> into the <u>openhammer</u>. | The word "step"<br><br>The words "into the" | Read these words slowly because they are part of a direction. |
| Scientists have found a new <u>stellus</u> in the sky. | The word "scientists"<br><br>The words "in the sky" | Read these words slowly because they tell important information. |

 **Practice Activity 2**

**Directions:** With a partner, read aloud the following sentences. Circle clues in each sentence that help you figure out the meaning of the made-up word.

1. Many years ago, a very wise goat lived in the land of <u>Turbuloo</u>.


2. Do you want to go with me to the <u>dweezlebry</u>?


**Lesson Practice begins on the following page.**

**Directions:** This passage is about a costume contest. Read the passage. Then, review the Reader's Checklist.

# *How to Win the Blue Ribbon*

It was down to the last three contestants. Who would win the blue ribbon? No one in the audience knew. Everyone was silent as the three walked onstage. A hot dog, a pumpkin, and a huge robot walked onto the stage. Each was a different dog in a costume!

Sneaky was a small, brown, skinny dog. Her costume made her look like a hot dog in a bun. She even had a little hat shaped like a dot of ketchup. Burton was a fat, short dog. He had a grumpy face. He was a perfect pumpkin in his orange costume. He also had a hat like a brown pumpkin stem. Both Sneaky and Burton were happily wagging their tails.

Then there was the third dog. You couldn't see his tail. You couldn't see his snout. You could see his ears and his big brown eyes peeking out of a robot head. He was huge. His name was Mondo.

"Hello, everyone," the judge said. "This year's Dog Costume Contest has been a great success. All the costumes were magnificent. These three were the best. I've had a hard time deciding who should win."

"If only I had a way to tell which dog was the best," the judge said. "Can Sneaky act like a hot dog? Can Burton act like a pumpkin? Can Mondo act like a robot?"

People in the crowd whispered and murmured. What if there was a tie? Which dog acted most like its character? How could a dog act like a hot dog?

Just then, Mondo barked. But in his robot head, his bark sounded funny. His bark sounded like a computer! He sat down and lifted up his big paw. It looked just like a robot putting out his hand. The whole audience broke out laughing. The judge smiled and clapped. It was as if Mondo knew he needed to act like a robot to win!

Mondo won the blue ribbon!

Good readers express themselves as they read. They read at a good rate and with a meaningful tone of voice. They also use clues in the text to help them better understand what they are reading and how to read it. They correct themselves as they read and reread when necessary.

**Read the Reader's Checklist below. Think about how you read the story. Check every box that is true about how you read the story.**

### Reader's Checklist

☐ I identified my purpose for reading.

☐ I paused briefly at commas (,).

☐ I stopped briefly at periods (.).

☐ I made my voice go up higher at question marks (?).

☐ I expressed feeling at exclamation points (!), such as strength, shock, fear, or anger.

☐ I said words within quotation marks (" ") the way the character would say them.

☐ I read at a good rate so that readers could understand what I was reading.

☐ I changed the rate I read depending on the details in the story.

☐ I used context clues in the story to read and understand unknown words.

**For every box you did not check, reread the story and make the needed changes.**

CCSs: RL.3.10, RI.3.10

# Lesson 4: What's the Main Idea?

Read the following article. It will help you to learn the tips in this lesson.

## *The Pony Express*

by Dexter Evans

In the mid-1800s, there were only two ways to get to California. One way was to sail around the tip of South America. That took a long time. Another way was to cross mountains and deserts on foot and in wagons. Either way, it was a hard and dangerous trip. But thousands of people moved west anyway.

California grew quickly and became a state in 1850. California was far from other parts of the United States. Mail service was very slow. It could take months for letters to be delivered. Nobody wanted to wait that long for news about their friends and families far away.

A man named William H. Russell ran a company that carried goods and passengers by wagon and stagecoach. In 1860, he hired a group of young men to ride fast horses from St. Joseph, Missouri, to Sacramento, California. Each rider would carry the mail for about 80 miles. He would stop at a relay station every 10 to 15 miles to get a fresh horse. When he reached his final stop (called a home station), he would give the mail to another rider. This new rider would carry the mail 80 miles to the next home station. It was like a relay race. This way, the mail could get to and from California much faster. The new mail service was called the Pony Express.

Eight Pony Express riders were on the job at any one time. There were also about 400 other Pony Express employees, including station keepers.

CCSs: RL.3.1, RL.3.10, RI.3.1, RI.3.2, RI.3.10

The Pony Express wanted riders who were not married because the job was so dangerous. The young men rode alone across Native American lands. It was a difficult job, but the mail almost always got through. It took the riders only eight or ten days to go from St. Joseph to Sacramento, instead of many weeks.

After 18 months, telegraph wires finally reached California. They made it easier to send and receive messages. The Pony Express went out of business. But it has been famous ever since as a colorful part of the history of the Old West.

 **TIP 1: The most important idea in a passage is called the main idea.**

Everything you read tells you something. A story tells you something. So does a poem and a math book. The **main idea** is what the passage or book is mostly about. Some passages have many important ideas. But there is only one *most* important idea.

Here are some of the important ideas in "The Pony Express":

- The trip west to California was hard and dangerous.

- William H. Russell started a service that carried the mail to and from California.

- Riding for the Pony Express could be a dangerous job.

- The Pony Express was used for only 18 months.

There is only one main idea in the whole story about the Pony Express. In this case, the main idea isn't given in a single sentence. You have to put together the details to figure it out.

1. What is the most important idea of the passage?

   A. It took a long time to sail around the tip of South America.

   B. Pony Express relay stations were about 15 miles apart.

   C. The Pony Express cut the time it took for mail to travel to and from California.

   D. William H. Russell ran a company that carried goods and passengers by wagon.

2. Go back to the story and underline details that tell about the main idea.

 **TIP 2:  Look for a sentence that tells the main idea.**

Sometimes a writer will come right out and tell you the main idea in a sentence. When you start reading a passage, look for any sentences that include the main idea.

Read the following passage. Then answer Numbers 3 through 5.

Spiderwebs are interesting and unusual things. Most spiderwebs are sticky because they are used to trap prey. But how do spiders walk on the webs without getting stuck? They have oily feet that slip and slide easily over the silk. Should a spider fall backward onto its own web, it will stick there like any other creature. Aargh!

Spiders weave webs.

There is a spider in Europe that spins a web so tiny, it's hard to see. It would barely cover a postage stamp.

If you went to India, however, you might see something quite the opposite of such a tiny web. One spider in India builds a web so big that it could cover half your classroom.

The water spider, as you might guess from its name, doesn't mind the water. But before crawling in, it moves its bell-shaped web through the water to collect air bubbles. When it has enough air bubbles, the spider heads below in its own little diving bell to look for food.

CCSs: RL.3.1, RL.3.10, RI.3.1, RI.3.2, RI.3.10

3. Which of these sentences tells the main idea of the passage?

   A. Spiderwebs are interesting and unusual things.

   B. One spider can build a web so big that it could cover half a classroom.

   C. One spider in Europe spins a web so tiny, it's hard to see.

   D. Spiders can walk on their webs without getting stuck.

4. What is the first paragraph mainly about?

   A. the way spiders walk on their sticky webs

   B. the tiny web made by a spider from Europe

   C. the huge web made by an Indian spider

   D. how the water spider uses its web to collect air bubbles

5. What is the last paragraph mainly about?

   A. the way spiders walk on their sticky webs

   B. the tiny web made by a spider from Europe

   C. the huge web made by an Indian spider

   D. how the water spider uses its web to collect air bubbles

**TIP 3:  Look for details that support the main idea.**

**Supporting details** give important information about the main idea. They help readers understand the main idea. In the passage about spiderwebs, the main idea is that webs are interesting and unusual. The details tell about different kinds of interesting and unusual webs.

The following paragraph is about Lena Horne. She was a talented African American singer and performer. This paragraph tells how Lena Horne was both talented and brave.

> Lena Horne was born in 1917. At a very young age, she was singing to packed houses of fans. She even sang in many popular movies at the time. Even though she was talented and very popular, she still was treated unfairly because she was African American. Sometimes she was not allowed to stay overnight in hotels where she was hired to sing! At the time, movies only showed African Americans in small roles as servants. Lena Horne didn't want to do those roles. She stood up for her rights. She chose not to take roles or jobs that she felt were unfair. Still, she had an amazing career! People around the world know her name and her voice.

6. What is the main idea of the paragraph?

   A. Lena Horne was a talented and successful singer and actress.

   B. African Americans were treated unfairly in everyday life and in movies.

   C. Lena Horne was a talented performer who stood up for her rights.

   D. People around the world like to listen to Lena Horne.

7. Look back at the paragraph about Lena Horne. Underline two details that support the main idea.

CCSs: RL.3.1, RL.3.2, RI.3.1, RI.3.2

 **TIP 4:  Put the main idea into your own words.**

Sometimes a writer just hints at the main idea. If you can't find a main idea sentence, try the following:

- Look for important details in the passage.

- Decide how the details work together.

- In your own words, tell how the details link together.

Your sentence should tell how the important ideas work together. The way they work together is what the passage is mostly about.

Read the following paragraph.

> Lukas was in the kitchen at his friend Jacob's house. Lukas always had fun hanging out with his friend Jacob. Today, they were playing a new guessing game. Lukas's hand was in a bowl of something, and he had to figure it out. Lukas couldn't see what was in the bowl because he had a blindfold on. He felt thin, worm-like things. They were slimy and sticky. He could stick his fingers into them like they were balls of string. Suddenly, he figured it out. "Spaghetti," Lukas shouted and grinned.

8.  What are Lukas and Jacob doing?

   A.  making dinner together in the kitchen

   B.  playing a guessing game with food

   C.  gathering a lot of worms in a bowl

   D.  playing with a bowl of wet string

9.  What does Lukas always have fun doing?

   A.  Lukas always has fun hanging out with Jacob.

   B.  Lukas always has fun wearing a blindfold.

   C.  Lukas always has fun when he is in Jacob's kitchen.

   D.  Lukas always has fun coming up with new games.

10. What does Lukas feel?

   A. Lukas feels thin, sticky, and slimy things.

   B. Lukas feels hungry and ready to eat.

   C. Lukas feels confused that he can't see.

   D. Lukas feels he does not like Jacob's new game.

11. Write the main idea of the paragraph in your own words.

_____

_____

_____

 **TIP 5: To find the main idea, try coming up with a title.**

A good title often tells the reader something about the main idea of the passage. Read the following paragraph. Think about the main idea.

> "Look into the sky," the principal told the students. "Is it a bird, a plane? No! It's our yearly kite-flying day!" The principal pointed into the spring sky over the schoolyard. There were a few teachers with kites flying high. The kites were beautiful. The students gasped and clapped.

Read Number 12. Think about which title best tells about the main idea of the paragraph. Cross out any answer choices that do not tell about the main idea.

12. Which of these titles best tells about the paragraph?

   A. "A Sad Day at School"

   B. "How to Make Your Own Kite"

   C. "A Spring Day Off from School"

   D. "Flying Kites at School"

Would the students clap at school if they felt sad? Does the principal tell students how to make their own kites? Would the students be in the schoolyard with the principal if they had a day off from school? The answers to these questions should help you figure out the main idea of the paragraph.

**Lesson Practice begins on the following page.**

**Directions:** This passage is about a goose that lays golden eggs. Read the passage. Then answer Numbers 1 through 5.

# *The Goose That Laid Golden Eggs*

retold by Alan Noble

A poor man lived in a tiny hut just outside a small village. No matter how much he worked, he barely earned enough money to buy food. Life was hard for such a poor fellow. Each night before he went to sleep, he told himself how much better life would be if only he had more money.

A poor man's goose lays golden eggs.

One cold spring morning, the man got ready to go out and gather firewood. He opened the door of his tiny hut. He nearly tripped over a goose sitting on a nest!

"Why, where did you come from?" the man asked.

Startled, the goose flew from the nest and circled high overhead.

Something in the bottom of the nest shone in the early morning light. The poor man <u>stooped</u> down to pick it up. It was an egg—but not just an <u>ordinary</u> egg. It was an egg made of pure gold. *What luck,* he said to himself, *for a poor man such as me to find riches such as this!*

Every morning, the goose laid another golden egg. In no time at all, the man became wealthy beyond his dearest dreams. He moved to a fine house and bought all the things he had ever wanted. His troubles seemed to be over.

But one thing nagged at him. The richer he became, the more riches he wanted. Soon, all he could think about was gold, gold, and more gold!

*Why should I get just one golden egg each day when I can get them all at once?* he wondered. Eagerly, the man killed the goose and cut it open to find ALL its eggs at once. Imagine his surprise when he found no eggs at all.

1.  **What is this story <u>mostly</u> about?**

    A.  how a poor man complains

    B.  how a poor man finds a goose

    C.  how a poor man gathers wood

    D.  how a poor man becomes greedy

2.  **Read this sentence from the story.**

    "The poor man stooped down to pick it up."

    **The word** *stooped* <u>most likely</u> **means the man**

    A.  bent over.

    B.  crawled.

    C.  sat down.

    D.  knelt.

3.  **The story says the egg was not ordinary. What does the word** *ordinary* **mean?**

    A.  special

    B.  beautiful

    C.  plain

    D.  heavy

4. **The title of this story is "The Goose That Laid Golden Eggs." What is another good title for this story?**

_____

_____

5. **Write the main idea of the story in your own words.**

_____

_____

_____

CCSs: RL.3.1, RL.3.2, RL.3.10, RI.3.1, RI.3.10

# Lesson 5: Don't Forget the Details

**Details** are bits of information that help you understand what is going on in a story.

We use details all the time. When we speak, we use details to explain what we mean. If you wanted to order a pizza, you would need to give some details. What would you like on your pizza? What size? What kind of crust? The answers to these questions are details. Without details, you may not get what you want.

Read this story. It will help you learn the tips in the lesson.

### *Doggone It*

Imagine that your dog, Scooter, ran through the backyard gate when your brother, Benji, took out the trash yesterday. You really love Scooter. You want her to come home. So you and Benji make 10 posters to hang up in your neighborhood. This is what the posters look like:

Pretty soon the telephone starts ringing. You quickly pick it up.
"Did you lose a cat?" the caller asks.
"No, we lost our dog," you say.
"Oh, sorry to bother you. I found a lost cat," the caller says and hangs up.
Oops. You and Benji take markers and run out to add the word *dog* to all the posters.

CCSs: RL.3.1, RL.3.2, RL.3.10, RI.3.1, RI.3.10

An hour later, the phone rings again. "I've found a lost dog that might be yours," the caller says.

"Scooter! You've found Scooter," you say. "Thanks! I really miss my little brown dog."

"Oh, I guess I don't have Scooter," the caller says. "This dog is big and has a red coat. I hope you find your dog." She hangs up.

"Come on, Benji," you say. "Here we go again." The two of you take your markers and add some more words to the posters.

It's supper time, and Scooter still hasn't returned home. You're really getting worried now. You walk outside and call, "Scooter! Come home, girl!" No luck. The phone rings, and you rush into the house to answer it.

"Hello, I've found a little brown dog in my yard. I wonder if it could be yours," the caller says. "Does your little brown dog have any markings on her?"

"Yes, she has a white spot on her nose, and the tip of her tail is white," you tell the caller.

"This dog has a white spot on her nose, and the tip of her tail is white," the caller says. "I think I've got your little brown dog."

"Please come over right away to find out if she is yours."

Your parents drive you and Benji to the caller's house. There you see that Scooter is tied to a tree with a long leash. "Scooter!" you yell as you run up to hug her.

Scooter gives you a great big lick on your cheek. She's happy to see you, too.

In the story about Scooter, you and Benji put up a poster about your lost dog. But there is a problem.

At first, the poster doesn't give much information about Scooter. It doesn't tell that she is a girl. It doesn't tell that she is little. It doesn't tell that she is brown. It doesn't even tell that she is a dog! The poster doesn't give any details about the missing dog.

1. Go back to the story. Reread it and underline details that tell you about Scooter.

2. The poster doesn't tell everything you know about Scooter. Add one more detail about Scooter to the poster at the bottom of page 47.

3. Where are Scooter's white spots?

    A. under her belly and between her eyes

    B. on her nose and the tip of her tail

    C. on her back and her front paws

    D. on all four paws and the tip of her nose

4. What detail is printed on the poster but is not given in the story?

    A. the dog's color

    B. the names of the dog's owners

    C. the phone number to call

    D. the size of the lost dog

5. How does adding details to the poster help in finding Scooter?

_____

_____

_____

_____

 **TIP 1: Use details to picture the story.**

Details are important in reading stories, just as they are in a "lost dog" poster. They help readers picture what is happening. They help us understand how things are alike and different. And they make the characters seem like real people.

Read this story, and then answer Numbers 6 and 7.

> Cullen wanted to play a prank on his older sister Sue. She was hard to scare. First, Cullen put a plastic snake on her bed. But she just threw it away. Then, Cullen put sugar in the salt shaker, so she put sugar on her popcorn. "The popcorn tastes good this way!" she said. Cullen went to the living room to think of a good prank. Suddenly, he felt something tickle his neck. He reached and felt a big hairy spider! Just then, he saw his sister behind him. She was holding a string with a plastic spider on the end. "Now that's funny," Sue said and giggled loudly.

6. Which of these is not a detail from the story?

A. Cullen used a plastic mouse.

B. Cullen used a plastic snake.

C. Cullen put sugar in the salt shaker.

D. Sue used a plastic spider.

7. Which of these best describes Cullen?

A. the older sister

B. the younger brother

C. a person who is hard to scare

D. someone who giggles loudly

CCSs: RL.3.1, RL.3.2, RL.3.10, RI.3.1, RI.3.10

**TIP 2:** **Find key words in the question or answer choices. Then look for them in the story.**

Most detail question and answer choices contain important words from the story. **Key words** are clues that can help you find answers in the passage. Look for key words in the next story.

Imagine that you weighed 85 tons and were about as tall as a four-story building. Would your legs get tired of supporting your heavy body?

Now, imagine the brachiosaurus. Its body was so heavy that it needed gigantic legs just to hold it up. Some scientists have compared the brachiosaurus's legs to the pillars that help hold up the roof of a building.

As big and bulky as they were, the legs of the brachiosaurus still got extremely tired. That was why the animal spent so much time standing in water. The water helped hold up the brachiosaurus's body. It probably soothed those aching legs, too!

The brachiosaurus was a tall, heavy dinosaur.

Look for the **bold** key words in Numbers 8 through 10. They will help you find the answers to the questions.

8. About how **tall** was a brachiosaurus?

_____

9. What part of a brachiosaurus has been **compared** to the **pillars** that help hold up the roof of a **building**?

_____

10. Why did the brachiosaurus spend so much time in the **water**?

    A. because it wanted to hide its big legs

    B. because it got very thirsty

    C. because it liked to swim

    D. because the water helped hold up its body

 **TIP 3: Retell the story in your own words to help put the events in order.**

Details tell readers what happens first, second, third, and so on. One of the best ways to keep a story straight is to pick out the important details. Then retell them in your own words. During a test, just tell it to yourself in your mind.

As you read the next story, look for the most important events.

    With a loud crack, Ashley hit the baseball with her Luis Gonzalez bat. It sailed high above the torn red cap on Daniel Maxwell's head. It grazed the leaves on a branch of the willow tree. It slid above the rickety board fence at the edge of Ashley's yard. And it kept going, right through Mr. Jackson's living room window.

Ashley hit the baseball into Mr. Jackson's living room.

    Ashley waited for the crash of glass. She waited for an angry yell. But Mr. Jackson didn't get mad. His window was open! The ball landed on a book in his lap. He stood up, leaned out the window, and threw the ball back over the fence.

11. Underline three important events in the story.

12. What happens last in the story?

    A. The ball lands in Mr. Jackson's lap.

    B. Ashley swings at the ball with her Luis Gonzalez bat.

    C. Mr. Jackson throws the ball back over the fence.

    D. The ball sails over Daniel Maxwell's head.

13. Retell the important events in your own words.

_____

_____

_____

_____

_____

 **TIP 4: Look for "order words" such as first, next, and last.**

Sometimes when you read a story, you'll see words that help you know the order in which events take place. Here are some "order words" to look for:

| | | | | |
|---|---|---|---|---|
| as | at last | first | last | now |
| after | before | following | later | then |
| at first | during | in addition | next | while |

 **TIP 5: Important details should tell you more about the main idea.**

Important details tell you the most about the main idea. They tell facts about something. Or they show what happens in a story. Other details make the writing interesting. But they are less important.

Some questions on a test ask which detail is the most important. Here's how to answer. First, think about the main idea. What is the passage mostly about? Then look at the choices. One choice will help to explain the main idea. That detail is the most important.

CCSs: RI.3.2, RL.3.10, RI.3.1

Answer this question about the brachiosaurus article in Tip 2 on page 50.

14.  What is the most important detail about the brachiosaurus in this story?

   A.  It weighed 85 tons.

   B.  It needed large legs.

   C.  It stood in water.

   D.  Its legs got tired.

Use the story about Ashley and the baseball on page 51 to answer this question.

15.  Which sentence is most important to the main idea of the story?

   A.  "It grazed the leaves on a branch of the willow tree."

   B.  "It slid above the rickety board fence at the edge of Ashley's yard."

   C.  "And it kept going, right through Mr. Jackson's living room window."

   D.  "The ball landed on a book in his lap."

**TIP 6: Use webs and other graphic organizers to list important details.**

A **graphic organizer** is a picture that puts information in order. A **web** is a graphic organizer. It links details to the main idea. The main idea is in the middle of the web. Lines connect the details to the main idea.

Here is a web about the pranks Cullen and his sister tried on page 49. The pranks are what are being described. It is in the middle of the web. The detail tells one prank described in the story.

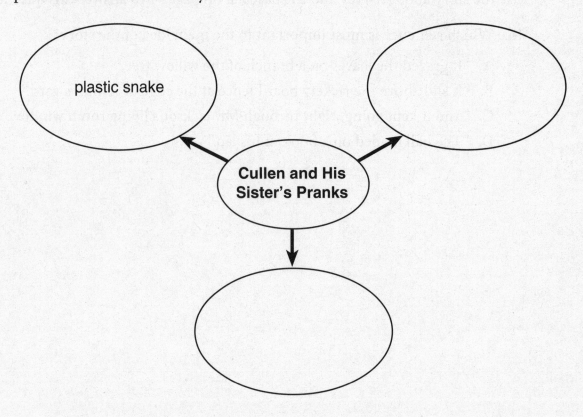

16. What other pranks did Cullen and his sister do? Add two more details about pranks they tried. You may look back at the story on page 49.

**Lesson Practice begins on the following page.**

**Directions:** This passage is about how two friends came up with the character Superman. Read the passage. Then, answer Numbers 1 through 5.

## How Superman Was Born

Jerry Siegel met Joe Shuster in 1931. The two boys were in high school. They became best friends and began making comic strips. Jerry wrote the stories, and Joe drew the pictures. They tried to sell their strips to newspapers. But no one wanted to buy them.

Jerry and Joe did not give up. Nothing could stop these two friends. They kept making comics. Soon, Jerry and Joe started their own magazine. It was called *Science Fiction*. The boys printed it at their school.

One night in 1934, Jerry stayed up all night. He was writing down ideas for a great new comic strip. It would mix space stories with mystery. Jerry took ideas from Flash Gordon, a character who had adventures in space. The new character would also fight bad guys like the Shadow, a radio show hero. Last, Jerry wanted a strongman like Hercules, the hero of many old stories.

The next morning, Jerry ran all the way to Joe's house. It was twelve blocks away! Jerry told his friend about his ideas. Joe began to make drawings of their new hero.

Both boys were excited about the character. But no newspaper wanted the strip. No one wanted it for a comic book. Still, the boys didn't give up. They found jobs writing and drawing other comic books. And they kept trying to sell their own idea.

Finally, Jerry and Joe got their chance. It came from Harry Donenfeld. He was starting a new comic book called *Action Comics*. Jerry and Joe sent their new comic strip to Donenfeld. He liked it.

It had taken four years, but they finally sold their idea. Soon, people all over the world would know the hero called Superman!

1.  **According to the passage, how did Jerry and Joe make their magazine?**

    A.  They sold it to a newspaper.

    B.  They printed it at school.

    C.  They found jobs making comics.

    D.  They sent it to Harry Donenfeld.

2.  **Which sentence is <u>most</u> important to the main idea of the passage?**

    A.  "Jerry Siegel met Joe Shuster in 1931."

    B.  "The two boys were in high school."

    C.  "Soon Jerry and Joe started their own magazine."

    D.  "It had taken four years, but they finally sold their idea."

3.  **Which sentence from the story contains order words?**

    A.  "They became best friends and began making comic strips."

    B.  "Joe began to make drawings of their new hero."

    C.  "No one wanted it for a comic book."

    D.  "Finally, Jerry and Joe got their chance."

4.  Jerry and Joe made their own magazine, called *Science Fiction*. What are some important details about the magazine *Science Fiction*?

_____

_____

_____

5.  In 1934, Jerry stayed up all night coming up with a new character. This graphic organizer is a web about the new character, called Superman. Complete the web with other details about the new character.

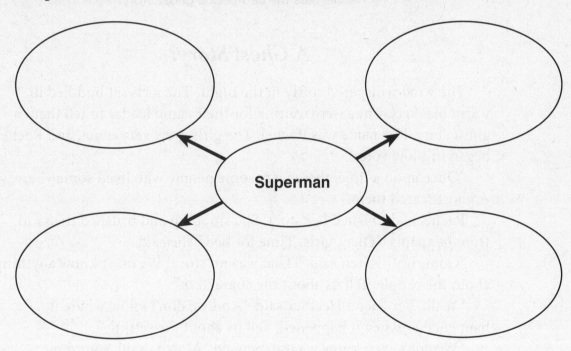

# Lesson 6: Tell Me a Made-Up Story

You probably tell or hear stories every day. You might tell your friends about a trip you took to the beach. Your dad might make you laugh with a made-up story about a bear in your closet. Made-up stories can be about other worlds, talking animals, all kinds of new things, and people just like you and me.

Rachel tells the campers a ghost story.

## *A Ghost Story?*

The wind whispered softly in the night. The girls sat huddled in warm blankets. They were waiting for their camp leader to tell them a ghost story. Her name was Rachel. The girls grew very quiet, and Rachel began in a low voice.

"Once upon a time, there were some people who lived somewhere. A ghost scared them."

Rachel had finished her story. She stood up and brushed the sand from her pants. "Okay, girls. Time for bed," she said.

"Come on!" Karen said. "That was no story! We don't know anything about the people. Tell us about the characters."

"Yeah," her friend Heather said. "And we don't know where it happened or when it happened. Tell us about the setting."

"We don't even know what happened," Marsha said, sounding disappointed. "Tell us about the plot."

**Two Kinds of Stories**

There are two main kinds of stories. First, there are stories that are made up by the author. We call this kind of writing **fiction**. You will learn about fiction in this lesson. Second, there are true stories about real people and real things. We call this kind of writing **nonfiction**. You will learn about nonfiction in Lesson 10.

**TIP 1:  A story has characters, a setting, and a plot.**

Made-up stories always have **characters**. Usually, the characters are people. But they can also be animals, such as the three little pigs. They can be strange creatures, like Dr. Seuss's Grinch. Characters might even be trees, cars, or trains that talk.

Made-up stories also give the reader a setting. The **setting** is the place and time of the story. The setting might be on a boat, in the mountains, at a ballpark, or on the moon. The story might take place today, a hundred years ago, or sometime far into the future.

Things have to happen in a story, too. These events make up the story's **plot**.

Read the following sentences. Then answer the questions that follow. Do these sentences tell mostly about characters, setting, or plot?

1.  Seven-year-old Hansel has a sister named Gretel.

    What does this sentence tell you about?

    A.  characters

    B.  setting

    C.  plot

2.  Seeing Cinderella dressed in rags, her fairy godmother uses magic to make a beautiful gown for her.

    What does this sentence tell you about?

    A.  characters

    B.  setting

    C.  plot

3.  The floor of the cave is cold, and its walls are wet.

    What does this sentence tell you about?

    A.  characters

    B.  setting

    C.  plot

4. Describe the setting, characters, or plot of one of your favorite stories.

_____

_____

_____

 **TIP 2:  Get to know the characters from what they say and do.**

You can get to know the characters in a story if you pay attention to details. You can learn what the characters look like, how they feel, and why they act a certain way. You may find out whether they are old or young, kind or mean, happy or sad.

Read this passage from a mystery story. Pay close attention to the details. Then answer the questions that follow.

Jody ran down the bike path beside Jackson Highway. She was frightened. Her long black hair streamed in the wind. A bright red book bag flopped wildly on her back. Her unbuttoned raincoat flapped in the wind like the wings of a giant yellow bird. When she got to Oak Street, she cut across Mr. Henry's lawn. Every now and then, she looked over her shoulder to see if Mrs. Parker was still following her.

Jody didn't stop running until she reached Elm Street and the safety of her own front steps. Nearly out of breath, she sat down, flipped the book bag onto her knees, and searched for a pencil. Not finding the pencil, she settled for a stubby green crayon and ripped a page from her third-grade spelling book. With shaking hands, she scribbled a quick note.

Michelle,
I can't meet you here after school today. I have to do something very important. See you tomorrow—I hope!

Jody C.

CCSs: RL.3.1, RL.3.3, RL.3.10

5. Which of the following best describes Jody?

    A. a police officer

    B. a neighborhood bully

    C. a third-grade student

    D. a friend of Mrs. Parker

6. Where does Jody live?

    A. on Elm Street

    B. on Oak Street

    C. near a bike path

    D. along Jackson Highway

7. Which word best tells how Jody feels?

    A. angry

    B. fearful

    C. cheerful

    D. grouchy

8. How does the author most likely want readers to feel?

    A. sad

    B. joyful

    C. amazed

    D. worried

9. In your own words, tell how Jody is dressed and what she looks like.

    _____

    _____

    _____

    _____

**TIP 3: Use details to picture the setting.**

The story's setting is the time and place an action happens. Longer stories and books may have many different settings. Again, look for details. They will tell you when and where the story takes place.

Read this fiction passage. Then answer the questions that follow.

> It was New Year's Eve, 1815. Captain Henry stood at the wheel of his sleek new steamboat. It was called the *Washington*. He looked at the Mississippi River from the wheelhouse atop his boat. The moonlight was shining on it. He watched carefully for shallow waters, sandbars, and tree snags. Bright sparks and heavy black smoke poured out of the boat's tall smokestacks. The soot-filled clouds trailed upriver and floated on the still night air. Steam hissed from the boilers. And, softly, the tinkle of a piano drifted up from the carpeted main cabin. *She's making good time,* the captain thought. *We should be in New Orleans before midnight.*

10. Which words best describe the night?

    A. clear and windy

    B. cloudy and windy

    C. moonlit and still

    D. cloudy and still

11. Which words best describe the setting of this passage?

    A. in New Orleans, Louisiana

    B. aboard a Mississippi steamboat

    C. near the piano in a carpeted main cabin

    D. near some sandbars and tree snags

12. What time of year does the action take place?

    A. summer

    B. fall

    C. winter

    D. spring

CCSs: RL.3.1, RL.3.3, RL.3.5, RL.3.7

 **TIP 4:  Find the problems in the story to learn about the plot.**

Stories wouldn't be very interesting without plots. Most of the time, the plot is about problems the characters face. These problems make the story exciting.

Most stories have a main problem and other, smaller problems. The main character may have a problem with another character, such as a parent, a bully, or a teacher. Or, the problem may be with a thing, such as a storm, a wild animal, or a broken bicycle.

Sometimes, the problem will be within the character. *Should I do this, or should I do that?* the character will wonder. Usually these problems will develop around the main idea of the story.

 **TIP 5:  Most stories follow a set pattern with the sequence of events.**

Many long stories are broken up into separate parts, called **chapters**. Each chapter focuses on an event or idea to gradually tell the story. Most stories and their chapters follow a pattern like this:

The **beginning** of a story usually introduces the characters and the setting. This is when you first learn about the characters. The beginning of a story also tells about the problems faced by the main character or characters.

The middle, or main chapters, of a story is called the **body**. This is when you'll learn more about the characters' problems, and the problems get bigger and bigger. The problems continue to grow until the story reaches its climax. The **climax** is the turning point in the story when the problems stop getting bigger and start to be solved.

The **end** of a story tells how the problem is solved or how the characters deal with their problems. The outcome of these problems is called the **resolution**.

13. Think of a fairy tale you know (such as "Cinderella," "Snow White," "Jack and the Beanstalk," "Hansel and Gretel," "The Three Billy Goats Gruff," "The Little Mermaid," "The Ugly Duckling," "Aladdin and His Lamp," or any other fairy tale you know and like). Then answer the following questions about it.

A. Which fairy tale have you selected?

_____

B. What do you learn about the main characters in the beginning of the fairy tale?

_____

_____

C. What did you learn about the main characters' problems at the beginning of the fairy tale?

_____

_____

D. What happens to the main characters during the middle of the fairy tale? How do the problems get bigger for the main character?

_____

_____

_____

E. How does the fairy tale end? How are the main characters' problems solved?

_____

_____

_____

_____

CCSs: RL.3.2, RL.3.10

 **TIP 6: Figure out the moral or lesson in the story.**

Many made-up stories teach a lesson or a moral. A **moral** is an idea about right and wrong actions. You can figure out the lesson or moral in a story by looking closely at the details.

Read the following paragraph.

## *The Rabbit and the Coyote*

A rabbit hopped into a field, where there was a coyote. The rabbit saw the coyote lick his lips. The coyote was hungry! So, the rabbit came up with a plan. "Oh, no, the sky is falling! Brother Coyote, come help. Lean against this rock, so the rock will hold up the sky! And I'll go fetch a stick to hold up the sky forever." So, the coyote rushed over and leaned against the rock as hard as he could. The rabbit hopped away to fetch the stick. The coyote leaned against the rock all day and all night. Still the rabbit did not come back. The coyote was very tired, but still he leaned up against the rock because he did not want the sky to fall.

14. A lesson in this story is that you can use your mind and wits to come up with a way to protect yourself from danger. Underline the details in the story that support this lesson.

15. Another lesson in this story is that fear can make you do things that do not make sense. Underline the details in the story that support this lesson.

16. Identify another lesson in this story. Write the lesson in your own words.

_____

_____

_____

**TIP 7: Identify the point of view of the characters in the story.**

**Point of view** describes the way that a character sees or thinks about something. It is the opinion and feelings the character has toward something. In the story "The Rabbit and the Coyote" on page 65, the rabbit and the coyote both have different points of view.

| Thing | Character | Point of View |
|---|---|---|
| *Rock* | Rabbit | The rabbit thinks of the rock as a way to trick the coyote. |
| | Coyote | The coyote thinks the rock holds up the sky. |
| *Rabbit* | Rabbit | The rabbit sees itself as smart and tricky. |
| | Coyote | The coyote sees the rabbit as food and then as having important information about the sky. |

17. Think about the coyote's point of view and opinions. What does the coyote think about itself?

_____

_____

18. Think about the rabbit's point of view and opinions. What does the rabbit think about the coyote?

_____

_____

 **TIP 8: Tell the difference between your point of view and the point of view of the characters in the story.**

As a reader, you can have a point of view about what is happening in a story. Your **point of view** is the way you see or think about the setting, characters, and events in a story. You can think of your point of view as your opinion.

You can have a different point of view from a character in a story. Often, a story is written so that you will have a different point of view on the events than the characters in the story.

**Practice Activity**

**Directions:** Read the paragraph. Then answer the questions.

> Tabitha was angry. It was her birthday. During breakfast, her mom didn't wish her a happy birthday. During school, none of her friends said anything either! She got off the school bus and stomped up to her front door. Just then, she heard a pop, crash, and giggle inside her house. *Could it be burglars*? she wondered. She peeked into the window and got a glance of her mom walking past. So, she opened the door. Tabitha decided she'd just spend the evening doing her homework in bed.

1. Which of the following is the setting of the story?

   A. the school bus      C. Tabitha's house

   B. the kitchen          D. a friend's house

2. Which best describes Tabitha?

   A. hardworking        C. hungry

   B. upset                D. curious

3. What does Tabitha think is making the pop, crash, and giggle noises?

   _____

   How does Tabitha plan to spend the evening?

   _____

4. What do you think is making the pop, crash, and giggle noises?

   _____

   How do you think Tabitha will spend the evening?

   _____

**Lesson Practice begins on the following page.**

**Directions:** This passage is about two sisters, Angie and Rosa. Read the passage. Then, answer Numbers 1 through 8.

from

# The Secrets of the Old Barn

by Robyn Winchell

Uncle Roberto said it would be the perfect way to spend a rainy afternoon. Angie and Rosa agreed. Their aunt and uncle's old barn hadn't been used for years, but the roof was good, and it didn't leak. Although it might be a little dusty, playing in the hayloft would be more fun than staying in the farmhouse for yet another rainy day.

The girls climbed toward the opening in the hayloft floor above them. They could hear the patter of rain peppering the roof and the low rumble of thunder in the distance. Pigeons cooed softly from the shadowy rafters high above them.

"This will be fun," Angie said as her head appeared above the loft floor. She scrambled to her feet in the dusty hay. Rosa followed her sister into the loft like a shadow.

Angie and Rosa explored the barn's hayloft.

"We can pretend we're mountain climbers," Rosa said, looking at the mounds of hay.

Just then, both girls froze. Something dark and furry hurried across the floor in front of them and disappeared into the hay.

"What was that?" Angie asked.

"Why, it looked like Beanie, Aunt Carmen's cat," Rosa said. "Aunt Carmen says she hasn't seen Beanie for more than two weeks."

"There she is again," Angie said, pointing to the cat, which was now lying on top of the straw, flicking its black tail from side to side.

The girls struggled over piles of loose hay, then bent down to pet the cat. It began to purr loudly. After a few minutes, Beanie stood, stretched, and disappeared into the hay once again. The girls began to hear soft noises coming from under the hay.

"What's making those sounds?" Angie asked.

"I don't know," Rosa replied.

The girls waited quietly, listening to the soft sounds coming from the hay. In a very short time, Beanie came back out. This time she was carrying a small spotted kitten in her mouth.

"Beanie's had kittens!" Angie said. "And look!" She pointed to a small tunnel in the hay. Four more blue-eyed kittens wobbled toward the girls.

"Oh, they're so cute!" Rosa said. She carefully picked up the littlest one. It squirmed in her hand and mewed a tiny cry.

Beanie gave a warning meow and batted at Rosa's hand with one paw.

"I think you'd better put it down," Angie said. "It doesn't look like Beanie thinks they're ready for company yet. Let's come back later and bring her a saucer of milk."

"Good idea," Rosa said, placing the baby kitten next to its mother.

"See you later, Beanie's babies," Angie said with a smile.

1. **What is the <u>best</u> title for this story?**

   A.  "The Rainy Day"

   B.  "Sisters Work Together"

   C.  "Angie and Rosa Visit Uncle Roberto"

   D.  "The Surprise in the Old Barn"

2. **What do the girls want to pretend?**

   A.  that they are mountain climbers

   B.  that they are at the playground

   C.  that they are baking a cake

   D.  that they are playing basketball

3. **What is the setting of the story?**

   A.  Uncle Roberto's house

   B.  a field of hay

   C.  Uncle Roberto's barn

   D.  in Rosa's tree house

4. **Which of the following <u>best</u> describes Rosa and Angie?**

   A.  sleepy

   B.  curious

   C.  funny

   D.  serious

5. **What color are the kittens' eyes?**

   A. green
   B. gray

   C. blue
   D. brown

6. **In the story, Rosa and Angie have a problem. They see something dark and furry in the barn, and they do not know what it is. How do they figure out what it is?**

   A. They freeze in the barn.

   B. They ask their Uncle Roberto.

   C. Aunt Carmen tells them what they've seen.

   D. They look at the hay and see Beanie.

7. **In the story, Rosa picks up one of Beanie's kittens. What is Rosa's point of view of the kitten?**

   _____

   _____

   _____

8. **In the story, Rosa picks up one of Beanie's kittens. What is Beanie's point of view of Rosa?**

   _____

   _____

   _____

   _____

# Lesson 7: Stories from Long Ago

As you learned in Lesson 6, the plot is what happens in a story. In most plots, the characters have a problem. The story is mostly about how the problem gets solved. Sometimes the story can be about how the problem *doesn't* get solved.

Often, characters will learn a lesson by solving or not solving the problem. The author introduces the lesson to share his or her ideas about how life works. So reading can sometimes teach you a lesson about life.

In this lesson, we will look at some of the kinds of stories that teach. We will learn where these stories came from and what they are usually about.

 **TIP 1:  Look at how the story ends to understand the lesson.**

Have you ever heard or read the story "Goldilocks and the Three Bears"? If you have, then you know that there is a lesson in the story. A young girl goes into a bear family's house. She sits in their chairs, eats their food, and tries out their beds. Then the bears come home and chase Goldilocks away. During this story, the author teaches a lesson. The lesson is that you should not use other people's things without asking.

 **TIP 2:  A folktale is a story from long ago.**

Thousands of years ago, there were no movies. There were no television shows and no video games. Most people didn't even have books! People told one another stories for fun. People also made up stories when they wanted to teach lessons. They told stories over and over so that everyone could learn them. Children would hear the stories, grow up, and then tell the stories to their children.

In time, people decided to put their stories on paper. We call these stories folktales. **Folktales** are stories from a long time ago. There are many different kinds of folktales. In this lesson, you will learn about five types: fairy tales, legends, fables, trickster tales, and tall tales.

CCSs: RL.3.2, RL.3.5

 **TIP 3:** **A fairy tale often shows good working against evil.**

In a **fairy tale**, evil characters often try to hurt good characters. They also try to make the good characters do bad things. A good character will then try to stop the evil ones from getting what they want. In the fairy tale "Jack and the Beanstalk," a mean giant tries to keep a young man named Jack from going home. Jack must figure out how to get away.

Also, a fairy tale often shows magic. For example, Jack uses magic beans to grow the tall beanstalk. In "Sleeping Beauty," a whole kingdom falls under a spell and sleeps for years.

Many fairy tales begin like this:

In "Jack and the Beanstalk," Jack chops down the beanstalk to keep away the giant.

Many fairy tales end like this:

*. . . happily ever after.*

When the heroes win and live "happily ever after," the lesson in the fairy tale is clear: good wins over evil.

1. What is the name of another fairy tale you know?

_____

2. Which of the following does not usually appear in a fairy tale?

   A. good characters

   B. magic

   C. science facts

   D. evil characters

 **TIP 4:  Fables often tell about animals acting like people to show us how we act sometimes.**

In the fable "The Lion and the Mouse," a lion catches a mouse to eat for his dinner. The mouse promises to help the lion if the lion will let him go. The lion does not think the tiny mouse could ever help him, but he lets the mouse go. Later, the lion steps on a thorn and cannot get it out of his paw. The little mouse comes along and takes the thorn out.

The lion doesn't eat the mouse for dinner.

The fable isn't only about a lion and a mouse. It is also about how people should help each other. It tells us that we may be surprised by who is able to help us.

"The Lion and the Mouse" is like most fables. **Fables** are simple stories that are really about big lessons. They make us see that we can often be selfish, foolish, or mean. Most characters in a fable are animals.

Some fables don't use animals, but they still make us see how we can sometimes act.

CCSs: RL.3.2, RL.3.5, RL.3.10

3. Which of these stories is most likely a fable?

    A. "The Hare and the Tortoise"

    B. "Penelope's Magic Pennies"

    C. "Why There Are Mountains"

    D. "Samira's Big Day at School"

People think that a man named Aesop was the first to tell many of the fables we know today. Nobody knows much about Aesop. He lived thousands of years ago. His stories have been told in many ways and in many countries. But the lessons stay the same. The following passage is one of Aesop's fables.

## The Ant and the Grasshopper

Many, many years ago, a grasshopper spent his summer singing in the tall grass. His neighbor, the ant, spent the same summer carrying tasty leaves to his home in the ground.

"Why do you work so hard?" asked the grasshopper. "It is too beautiful outside. Summer is the time to play."

The ant kept working. He was not going to let the grasshopper upset his plan of action.

The ant works while the grasshopper plays.

Soon fall came, and after that came winter. Cold winds blew across the sea, chilling the earth. The grasshopper found himself hungry and in need of some food.

"Help me, I'm hungry," the grasshopper said to the ant.

"Didn't I see you during the summer, singing instead of working?" asked the ant.

"Yes, that was me," said the shivering grasshopper.

"You sang all summer," said the ant. "You should dance all winter."

4. What is the most important lesson this fable teaches?

    A. You should always share your things with others.

    B. You can't always count on friends when you need them.

    C. You must always plan ahead in case hard times come.

    D. You should relax and enjoy the good times while you can.

## TIP 5: Trickster tales tell about characters that fool others.

In **trickster tales**, one character tricks another character to teach him or her a lesson. The character that gets tricked is usually mean or too proud. The trick that is played gives the "bad" character a taste of his or her own medicine. In many trickster tales, there is also a "good" character who does not fall for the trickster's trick.

Tricksters appear in folktales from all around the world. Often the trickster is an animal, such as a fox, a crow, or a rabbit. People thought these animals were clever, so they based their tricksters on them. Some modern-day tricksters are Bugs Bunny and Captain Jack Sparrow from *Pirates of the Caribbean*.

## TIP 6: Legends show what it means to be a hero.

Another kind of folktale is called a legend. **Legends** tell about the lives of brave, strong characters that are often based on real people. The heroes of these stories do great things that show us the best parts of ourselves.

"Robin Hood" is an English legend. In the story, a man named Robin Hood steals from the rich to give to the poor. He never keeps what he steals for himself. Robin Hood is very brave and very generous. He teaches us that these can be our strengths, too.

There may have been a real Robin Hood. There may not have been. Not everyone agrees. For many legends, we cannot be sure that there was a real person who did the things in the story. Usually, though, at least some part of the legend is true. For example, in "Robin Hood," the sheriff and king are based on real people.

CCSs: RL.3.2, RL.3.5

 **TIP 7: Tall tales tell about larger-than-life characters.**

**Tall tales** tell about characters that are stronger or faster than people are in real life. The main character in a tall tale solves his or her problems by doing things that no real human could do.

In the tall-tale story of John Henry, there is a contest to see which can dig through a mountain faster: John Henry or a machine. John Henry is a very strong man. He hammers his way through the mountain all by himself. In the end, John Henry beats the machine and wins the contest. The story teaches us that not giving up is a great strength.

Let's compare Robin Hood to John Henry. The difference between Robin Hood and John Henry is the difference between a legend and a tall tale. Both characters may or may not be based on real people. Their stories both tell us good things about ourselves. But in a legend, the characters seem real. And in a tall tale, the characters are superhuman. Robin Hood could have easily stolen items and money to help poor people. But do you think John Henry could have really hammered through a mountain by himself?

5. Write the beginning of a tall tale. The main character could be similar to someone you know.

_____

_____

_____

_____

_____

_____

_____

_____

**TIP 8:** **Writers compare things by using similes (saying one thing is** *like* **or** *as* **another).**

Writers of all stories—made-up stories, fairy tales, fables, and others—use fun and interesting language. Sometimes writers use literal language. **Literal language** is language that means exactly what you'd think. For example, "the balloon was blue" means that the balloon was blue in color.

Often, though, writers often try to help us see everyday things in new ways. One way they do this is through figurative language. **Figurative language** suggests extra meaning. Similes and metaphors are forms of figurative language. They use one thing to make us think of another thing. When writers say one thing is *like* or *as* another, they are using a **simile**.

For example, a writer may say that the princess took a bite of an apple so soft <u>like</u> a rose or that the apple was <u>as red as</u> a rose. Most people don't think of roses when they take a bite out of an apple.

But comparing an apple to a rose helps us see how the two things are alike.

6.  Read these sentences taken from different stories. Circle the examples of literal language. Underline the examples of figurative language.

| | | |
|---|---|---|
| They left a trail of bread crumbs. | The beanstalk was as tall as a tree. | The fire was hotter than the sun. |
| She lived in a castle. | Her hair shone as bright as a star. | The baby bird grew big and strong. |

7.  Finish the following sentence by comparing a soft bed to something else. You'll be using a simile.

    This bed is as soft as _____

8.  Now write your own sentence comparing one thing to another.

    _____

    _____

CCSs: RL.3.4, RL.3.10, L.3.5a

Why would a writer go to the trouble of using figurative language and making up similes? Because they make poems and stories more fun to read. They help us use our imaginations to see the world in ways we never thought of before.

Do you know these lines by Ann and Jane Taylor?

from

### *The Star*

Twinkle, twinkle, little star
How I wonder what you are!
Up above the world so high,
Like a diamond in the sky.

9. The poet uses a simile to compare a little star to

A. a child.

B. the sky.

C. the world.

D. a diamond.

CCSs: RL.3.4, RL.3.10, L.3.5a

 **TIP 9:** Writers compare things by using metaphors (saying one thing really *is* another thing).

Sometimes, the writer says that one thing really *is* another thing. This is called a **metaphor**. A metaphor is another type of figurative language. In the following poem, the author uses a metaphor to describe a bike.

### My Rocket Ship

by Mike Acton

I have a little rocket ship
  With shiny spokes and chrome—
And ten speeds I can change at will
  When I blast off for home.
I wear my helmet fastened tight
  And lean into the wind,
When we are streaking through the stars
  Or up the driveway's bend.

The poet does not say that his bike is *like* a rocket ship. He uses a metaphor to suggest that the bike *is* a rocket ship.

10. In the box that follows, draw a picture about the poem. Show how the speaker's bike is a rocket ship.

CCSs: RL.3.4, RL.3.10, L.3.5a

Imagine you are lying on your back and looking up into the afternoon sky as you read the next poem. Then answer Numbers 11 through 13.

## Clouds
### by Christina Rossetti

White sheep, white sheep,
 On a blue hill,
When the wind stops
 You all stand still.
When the wind blows
 You walk away slow.
White sheep, white sheep,
 Where do you go?

11. The "white sheep" are really

    A. trees.

    B. kites.

    C. clouds.

    D. sheep.

12. What is the "blue hill"?

    A. the sky

    B. a meadow

    C. a flower

    D. a mountain

13. When the poet says, "You walk away slow," she means that

    A. the sun is crossing the sky.

    B. the sheep are looking for grass.

    C. clouds are moving across the sky.

    D. flowers are blowing in the wind.

**TIP 10:** Sensory words are words that excite our senses of sight, hearing, touch, taste, and smell.

The word *sensory* has to do with our senses. **Sensory words** are words that help us to see, hear, feel, smell, or taste what the author is writing about. Here are some examples of sensory words doing their job to help you better understand what the author is talking about.

**sight** — The dew sparkled in the grass like ten million jewels.

**hearing** — The airplane thundered from the runway and roared into the night sky.

**touch** — The kitten's tongue felt like warm sandpaper as it licked the milk from my finger.

**taste** — Uncle Ned's homemade chili tasted like a burning cactus.

**smell** — Mom's pie filled the air with smells of cinnamon, apples, and freshly baked crust.

14. Write a sentence using sensory words that tells about how something looks (sight).

_____

_____

_____

**Lesson Practice begins on the following page.**

**Directions:** This passage is about how animals save the sun. Read the passage. Then answer Numbers 1 through 8.

# *How the Sun Was Saved*

adapted from a Siberian folktale

Once upon a time, evil spirits stole the sun from the animals of the north land. The birds and the beasts had to find their food in the dark. At last, they called a meeting.

A wise raven spoke. He was so old that his voice squeaked like a rusty door. "We cannot live without the sun. I say we send the bear to get it. He is big and strong."

An old owl did not agree. "Yes, he is strong, but as soon as he finds food, he will forget about the sun."

"Then let us send the wolf," said the raven. "He is strong and quick."

Again the old owl did not agree. "He is greedy. As soon as he finds his first deer, he will forget the sun."

A tiny mouse said, "Send the rabbit. He's the best runner."

The old owl agreed. "And he is not selfish. He may catch the sun."

So the animals sent the rabbit on a long trip. At the bottom of the earth, the rabbit found a crack of light. He went through the crack, and there he saw a great ball of fire resting in a stone pot.

The rabbit held the great golden ball of fire. As he took it through the crack, the evil spirits started chasing him. The rabbit ran as fast as he could. Just as the evil spirits were about to catch him, the rabbit kicked the ball of fire into two pieces. He kicked the smaller piece into the sky, where it became the moon. He kicked the larger piece into another part of the sky, where it became the sun.

The earth brightened so that the evil spirits had to hide. They were never seen again. All the birds and beasts of the north land sang to honor the rabbit who had saved the sun.

1. **This passage is a folktale because**

   A.  it is about a real event.

   B.  it is about a real person.

   C.  the characters are animals.

   D.  it has lines that rhyme.

2. **What is the <u>main</u> problem in this folktale?**

   A.  The wolf hunts the deer.

   B.  The animals do not have light.

   C.  The bear is forgetful.

   D.  The rabbit kicks the ball of fire.

3. **What is the <u>main</u> setting of this folktale?**

   A.  in the city

   B.  in the desert

   C.  in the north

   D.  on an island

4. **What animal did the animals first suggest should go get the sun?**

   A.  the bear

   B.  the owl

   C.  the rabbit

   D.  the wolf

5. **What lesson does this folktale teach?**

   A.  Animals can solve many problems.

   B.  It is good to be brave and unselfish.

   C.  Wolves can be very greedy animals.

   D.  Animals in the north do not have much sun.

6. **Read this line from the folktale.**

"He was so old that his voice squeaked like a rusty door."

**What is this an example of?**

A. simile

B. metaphor

C. rhythm

D. rhyme

7. **Which line from the folktale appeals to our sense of sight?**

A. "At last, they called a meeting."

B. "I say we send the bear to get it."

C. "So the animals sent the rabbit on a long trip."

D. "The rabbit held the great golden ball of fire."

8. **The bear, the wolf, and the rabbit are described in the folktale using literal language. Write a simile or metaphor to describe each.**

_____

_____

_____

_____

_____

_____

# Lesson 8: Words That Sing

**Poetry** is a special kind of writing. It can be about made-up people and places. Poetry can also be about something that really happened. Poets use words that guide our senses. They help us imagine sights, sounds, feelings, tastes, and even smells as we read.

 **TIP 1:  Look for the poem's main idea.**

When you first read a poem, you may not understand every word. Don't worry. After you read it the first time, just ask yourself, *What is this poem mainly about?*

Once you know the poet's main idea, you can read the poem again to help you understand the meaning. Rereading the poem will help you understand it better. It will also help you see the special ways that poets put words together.

Read this poem all the way through. Then answer Number 1 on the next page.

## *Mother Says It's Time to Sleep*

by Juanita Kopaska

It's wrong that I am off to bed
When skies are blue and sun is red,
But Mother says it's time to sleep.
I wish she'd tell my mind and feet!

5    Although my eyes are getting tired,
My mind and feet are both on fire!
I want to climb the backyard gate
And watch the brown cows as they wait

For Dad to milk them one by one.
10   But for me, the day is done.
My eyes hum softly, "Time to dream—"
While feet and mind say, "Run!" and "Scream!"

But Mother says it's time to sleep.
She doesn't want to hear a peep.
15   And so it's into bed I climb,
Although it's just past suppertime.

CCSs: RL.3.5, RL.3.10, RF.3.4b

1.  What is the main idea of "Mother Says It's Time to Sleep"?

_____

_____

_____

 **TIP 2:  Notice how the lines are grouped.**

Poets usually break their poems into different parts: lines and stanzas. A **line** is a set of words, but not necessarily a sentence. A **stanza** is a group of lines. Stanzas in poetry are like paragraphs in other kinds of writing.

As you learned in Lesson 3, you can change how you read to express different feelings. You can pause at punctuation marks, change your voice to express feeling, and so on. When you read poetry aloud, you may be tempted to pause at the end of each line. Only pause when you see a punctuation mark, such as a comma or a period. When you get to the end of a line and there is no punctuation, do not pause. Continue reading to the next line.

Poets use stanzas to break up ideas. The stanzas in a poem often have the same number of lines.

Look at the poem on the next page, but don't read it yet. Use it to answer Number 2.

2.  How many stanzas are in the poem "Barry and Larry"?

A.  1

B.  2

C.  3

D.  6

**TIP 3:  Look for the poem's theme.**

The **theme** is the idea that links the poem to all people. It is a message for the reader. Answer any of these questions to figure out the poem's theme:

- Is the poem about characters and their actions? What is the most important thing the characters do?

- Does the poem make you feel a certain way? What is that feeling?

- Does the poem teach a lesson? What is that lesson?

Read the following poem. Then answer Numbers 3 and 4 on the next page.

# *Barry and Larry*

by Mickey Toom

Barry liked hiking
And Larry liked biking
And both liked to go to the zoo.
When Larry had candy,
5    Then Barry had candy.
What was one's, was the other one's, too.

When Barry caught mumps,
Larry got the same lumps,
And each had the face of a clown.
10    So Larry gave Barry
A gift to help carry
Him through till the swelling went down.

Larry liked airplanes
And Barry liked old trains.
15    Together, they liked to play ball.
But it ended when Larry
Saw his best friend Barry
Hold hands with a *girl* at the mall!

CCSs: RL.3.5, RL.3.10

3. What is the main idea of the poem?

    A. Larry and Barry both get sick with the mumps.

    B. Larry and Barry always share their candy.

    C. Larry likes airplanes, and Barry likes old trains.

    D. Larry and Barry are friends until Barry meets a girl.

4. What is the poem's theme?

    A. Friends should have the same hobbies.

    B. Family should always come first.

    C. When friends are close they share sickness.

    D. Don't let love get in the way of friendship.

 **TIP 4: Understand details in the poem.**

Poets may not say exactly what they mean. They want the reader to figure it out. So, reading a poem is kind of like solving a puzzle. You have to look for clues in the details. Put clues together to figure out the poem's meaning.

If something confuses you in a poem, it can be a good idea to just keep reading. You may find clues later in the poem.

5. Read these lines from "Barry and Larry."

    When Barry caught mumps,

    Larry got the same lumps,

    And each had the face of a clown.

    In these lines, which words could be used in place of "the face of a clown"?

    A. sad eyes

    B. a swollen face

    C. lots of makeup

    D. a big smile

**Lesson Practice begins on the following page.**

**Directions:** This poem is about different clocks. Read the poem. Then answer Numbers 1 through 5.

# *Clocks*

by Robyn Winchell

My grandpa has a great big clock
Against the parlor wall.
Its face is larger than a plate,
Its case is proud and tall.

5    Its long lone arm swings back and forth
And gives a swish and sigh
Each time the gears inside go "tick"
Or "tock" as I walk by.

My grandma has a china clock,
10   Pretty and very small.
Though busy on the fireplace
It's hardly seen at all.

The room is always full of sound—
The big clock's noisy gong
15   And, muffled, from its mantle place,
The small clock's tiny song.

Whenever Grandpa's mighty clock
Booms out its boastful sound,
The little clock just softly clucks
20   As if to say, "Pipe down."

This is an example of a grandfather clock.

1.  **This poem is <u>mostly</u> about how two clocks are**

    A.  noisy.

    B.  different.

    C.  alive.

    D.  beautiful.

2.  **How many stanzas are in the poem "Clocks"?**

    A.  4

    B.  5

    C.  10

    D.  20

3.  **Which detail is <u>most</u> important to the meaning of the poem?**

    A.  Grandpa's clock is against the wall.

    B.  Grandma's clock is on the fireplace.

    C.  The big clock's arm swishes as it moves.

    D.  The big clock makes loud ringing sounds.

4.  **In this poem, the speaker <u>most likely</u> feels the two clocks are**

    A.  funny.

    B.  scary.

    C.  boring.

    D.  precious.

5.  **Different stanzas focus on different ideas or characters. Look at stanzas 1 and 3. How are these stanzas <u>alike</u> and how are they <u>different</u>?**

    _____

    _____

    _____

    _____

# Lesson 9: Stories for the Stage

**Dramas** are stories people act out in front of other people or in front of a camera. Some examples of drama are plays, TV shows, and movies. In this lesson, you will learn about drama and how it is different from other kinds of fiction stories.

 **TIP 1:  See how the play is divided into acts and scenes.**

Have you ever picked up a really big book? It was probably divided into chapters. Plays are divided into parts, too. These parts are called acts and scenes. **Acts** are the largest parts of a play. You may think of acts as the chapters. Most plays have up to five acts.

**Scenes** are smaller parts of a play. Usually, two or more scenes are in each act. You may think of scenes as parts of a chapter.

1.  Which statement is true?

    A.  Acts are divided into scenes.

    B.  Scenes are divided into acts.

    C.  All plays are divided into scenes only.

    D.  All plays are divided into acts only.

 **TIP 2:  Plays do not tell how things look as much as stories do.**

In stories, authors give you a lot of information. They may tell you what characters look like. They may tell you how the characters walk, what they wear, and what they feel.

This audience is waiting for the curtains to open and the play to start.

Plays are a little different. Writers do not have to give as many details because the play takes place in front of people's eyes. The people watching can already see how the characters look, dress, and act. The people can also see what the setting looks like. The writer tells a little about the set at the beginning of each act and scene.

CCSs: RL.3.5, RL.3.10

For example, look at this explanation of a set. Then answer Number 2.

*(Setting: present day. The curtain opens on a child's bedroom. The walls are covered with music posters. The floor is covered with books and clothes. The bed is unmade, and a giant bear is standing in the middle of the room.)*

2. What is the setting of this play?

    A. a child's bedroom in the past

    B. a child's bedroom in the present day

    C. a messy classroom in the past

    D. a messy classroom in the present day

 ## TIP 3: Check the cast list.

The **cast** is a list of all the characters in a play. Sometimes, the actors' names are listed next to the characters they play. Usually, the cast list is found at the beginning of a play.

Look at this example. Then answer Number 3.

**CAST OF CHARACTERS**

**ERIC**, a soldier

**INGA**, Eric's younger sister

**TOR**, Eric's uncle

**BRENDA**, Eric's aunt

**COLBY**, Eric's friend

3. Who is Colby in this play?

    A. an uncle

    B. a brother

    C. a friend

    D. a soldier

Three of the characters from this play are onstage.

**TIP 4: Read what the characters say carefully.**

A lot of talking occurs in a play. After all, that is how most of the story is told! **Dialogue** is the words characters say to one another. The dialogue of a play is very important. It tells the audience what the characters feel and think.

Read this section from a play. It shows characters having a dialogue.

> **ERIC:**   We must get ready for battle. Colby, where is my shield?
>
> **COLBY:** I don't know. Where did you have it last?
>
> **INGA:**   (*rolls eyes*) Don't tell me you've lost your shield again, Eric!
>
> **ERIC:**   It's not really lost. (*sighs*) It's just hiding for the moment.

4. Which characters are talking in this scene?

   A. Eric, Colby, and Inga          C. Colby and Inga

   B. Inga and Eric                        D. Eric, Inga, and Brenda

 **TIP 5: Stage directions tell the actors how to move on the stage.**

Look back at the dialogue in Tip 4. Did you notice the words *rolls eyes* and *sighs*? Are those words the actors are supposed to say?

No. These words are stage directions. **Stage directions** give instructions to the characters or tell about the set. They can tell about things such as lighting and scenery. They may also tell actors how to move onstage. Stage directions are usually placed inside parentheses ( ) and printed in *italic type*.

---

**Drama Words**

**act** — a large part of a play that is usually made up of smaller parts called *scenes*

**cast** — the characters in a play and the actors who play those characters

**dialogue** — the spoken words of a play

**playwright** — the author of a play

**scene** — a part of the story with its own setting

**set** — the stage and scenery used in a play

**setting** — the place and time in which the action takes place

**stage directions** — instructions that tell the actors where and how to move

---

## Lesson Practice begins on the following page.

**Directions:** This story is about a poor shoemaker and his wife. Read the story. Then answer Numbers 1 through 10.

# The Elves and the Shoemaker

by Jakob and Wilhelm Grimm
adapted for the stage by Mike Acton

## CAST OF CHARACTERS:

**FRANZ**, a shoemaker          **MAN**, a customer
**MAMA**, his wife

## Scene 1

*(SETTING: The workshop of FRANZ, a poor shoemaker. There is a bare window at the rear of the stage. There is also an open closet door and a door to the living area on the left of the stage, an entry door with a signal bell on the right side, and a shoemaker's workbench with a three-legged stool near the center of the stage. A rocking chair sits near the living-area door. It is night. A candle burns on the workbench. FRANZ sits on his stool, using a large pair of scissors to cut leather for a pair of shoes. He peers over his glasses and speaks to his wife, who is rocking slowly.)*

**FRANZ:** Mama, this is the last of our leather. I will finish cutting it tonight and make a pair of shoes in the morning. If I can sell those shoes, we can buy food.

**MAMA:** But Franz, what are we going to do tonight? We have nothing but a few cups of flour. And that *(she points to the workbench)* is our last candle.

**FRANZ:** I know, Mama. We'll have to go to bed hungry tonight. I hope I can sell a pair of shoes tomorrow. *(Picks up the candle and walks toward the rocking chair)* Come along, Mama. Let's sleep now.

*(The couple moves slowly through the living-area door. Stage lights dim, then go off. The candle flickers in the living area for a few seconds, then goes out. Darkness.)*

## Scene 2

*(Slowly the lights come up and FRANZ appears in a nightgown and nightcap, holding a burning candle. He walks up to the workbench, yawning.)*

**FRANZ:** *(Stares at a completed pair of shoes sitting on the workbench)* What is this? What is this thing I am seeing? *(Picks up each shoe, one at a time, and looks at them closely)* Such beautiful stitches. Masterful! This is the work of a skilled cobbler! Wonderful work! *(Loudly)* Mama! Mama! Come here. Come look what I've found!

**MAMA:** *(Rushing toward the workbench in her nightgown)* What is it, Franz? You'll wake the whole neighborhood. What have you found?

**FRANZ:** Look, Mama. These shoes. Somebody has finished them for me. And Mama, it's the work of a master cobbler. Look, see for yourself.

**MAMA:** They are very nice, Papa. But now we need to sell them.

*(The entrance door opens, its bell rings, and a well-dressed customer enters.)*

**MAN:** Good morning, shoemaker. Still in your nightclothes, I see. Strange bunch, you cobblers! *(FRANZ pulls off his nightcap and bows.)* Oh well! Let's get on with it. I need a pair of shoes in a hurry.

**MAMA:** *(Sitting in her rocking chair)* Franz makes the finest pair of shoes in all the village.

**FRANZ:** Why, thank you, Mama. Please excuse my nightclothes, sir. I have not had time to dress. If you would like them, I have just finished making some shoes. *(Hands the shoes to the customer)* Try them on. Here, have my seat.

**MAN:** *(Seating himself on FRANZ'S stool and trying on the shoes)* These shoes are perfect! I can tell you put them together carefully. I'll buy them. How much do they cost?

**FRANZ:** Four coins, sir.

**MAN:** Here. Take eight coins. This is a fine pair of shoes. I'm sure they are worth more than four coins. Thank you. I will be back for more shoes another day. Good-bye.

**FRANZ:** Thank you, sir. Good day. *(Customer exits)* Mama, Mama, we have enough money to buy food and leather for at least two more pairs of shoes. We owe our success to an unknown master shoemaker and a generous customer. *(They hug each other in happiness.)*

*(Curtain)*

1. **"The Elves and the Shoemaker" is what kind of writing?**

   A. a story

   B. a poem

   C. a drama

   D. an article

2. **How many characters speak in "The Elves and the Shoemaker"?**

   A. 1

   B. 2

   C. 3

   D. 4

3.  **How many scenes are in "The Elves and the Shoemaker"?**

    A.  1

    B.  2

    C.  3

    D.  4

4.  **What is Franz's <u>biggest</u> problem at the beginning of the play?**

    A.  He needs better tools.

    B.  He needs food and candles.

    C.  He needs to get more leather.

    D.  He needs to buy a new rocking chair.

5.  **What is the setting?**

    A.  an attic

    B.  a bedroom

    C.  a basement

    D.  a workshop

6.  **How are Franz and Mama <u>alike</u>?**

    A.  They both are rich.

    B.  They both make shoes.

    C.  They both want to keep the new shoes.

    D.  They both are happy to sell the new shoes.

7. How much does the customer pay Franz for the shoes?

   A.  2 coins

   B.  4 coins

   C.  6 coins

   D.  8 coins

8. Which of the following is a stage direction from "The Elves and the Shoemaker"?

   A.  adapted for the stage by Mike Acton

   B.  Mama, this is the last of our leather.

   C.  *(she points to the workbench)*

   D.  These shoes are perfect!

9. Different scenes can happen at different times. Look at Scenes 1 and 2. What is one difference between when these scenes happen?

   _____

   _____

   _____

   _____

10. Different scenes focus on different actions or characters. Look at Scenes 1 and 2. How are these scenes <u>alike</u> and how are they <u>different</u>?

    _____

    _____

    _____

    _____

    _____

# Lesson 10: Tell Me a True Story

Read this passage. It will help you learn the tips in this lesson.

## The Truth About Snakes
### by Todd Hamer

**How long are snakes?**

The longest snake ever measured was an anaconda from South America. It was 37 feet long, about the length of a school bus. The Braminy blind snake, found in many countries including the United States, grows to be only six inches long. This is only as long as a fork or knife! You can see how big that is by checking a ruler. Most common snakes are between one foot and five feet in length.

**Where do snakes live?**

Snakes live in four main places: (1) Many snakes can be found on land. They often live under rocks or in tall grass. (2) Others live in cool caves or burrow in the moist soil like worms. (3) Some snakes live in trees. They have strong tails that grip branches and keep them from falling. (4) Still others live in rivers, swamps, or oceans. Snakes that live in water are very good swimmers.

**What do snakes eat?**

Snakes are an important part of the food chain. Some snakes eat mice, rats, and insects. They also eat frogs and small birds. Larger snakes eat slightly larger animals—including other snakes.

**Do snakes have enemies?**

Snakes have many enemies. Lizards, birds of prey, and alligators eat snakes. Cobra snakes live in most of Central Asia. They have a deadly enemy called the mongoose. The mongoose is a small mammal that is very fast. It can jump out of the way of a cobra's strike, then jump back in and quickly bite the snake.

A snake's two greatest enemies are other snakes and people. Snakes kill each other for food and to protect or take over new territory. People kill snakes for many unfair reasons. The main reason is probably fear. People sometimes think that all snakes are dangerous, but only a few types of snakes in the world are actually dangerous. People usually fear snakes because they don't understand them. Maybe now that you know a little more about snakes, you can help other people understand them, too.

**TIP 1:** Any story or article that is not made up by the writer is called nonfiction.

Many stories tell about things made up by the writer. But there are other kinds of writing that tell true stories about real people, real places, real things, and real happenings. You can find true stories in newspapers, in magazines, in books, and even on the Internet. This kind of writing is known as **nonfiction**.

The passage you just read, "The Truth About Snakes," contains facts about snakes and how they live. History books, geography books, travel guides, and cookbooks are all examples of nonfiction.

There are many types of nonfiction books.

1. Which of these books is fiction?

   A. *The Life of Abraham Lincoln*
   B. *The Dragon Under Johnny's Bed*
   C. *Webster's New World Dictionary*
   D. *The How-To Book for Bicycle Repair*

2. Which of these books is nonfiction?

   A. *Alice's Flying Bicycle*
   B. *Children's Favorite Fairy Tales*
   C. *Julio and His Magic Flute*
   D. *How Clouds Are Formed*

Now, read this passage. It will help you learn the tips in this lesson.

# Snake Champions

In the country of India, there are many different kinds of snakes. Some are not very dangerous. But some of the most dangerous snakes in the world also live in India. These snakes are the cobra and the viper. They are known for being quick and strong. Their bites are very painful. A person could get very sick or even die if bitten by a cobra or a viper.

### Snakebites

A person bitten by a cobra or a viper needs to see a special doctor right away. The person will need antivenom right away. Antivenom is a special type of medicine. It is the most helpful medicine for poisonous snakebites. Not all snakebites are poisonous, so every person bitten by a snake does not need antivenom.

But making antivenom is hard. First, a scientist needs venom from an actual snake. Then, the scientist uses the venom to make antivenom. The scientist changes the venom into medicine. Finally, the antivenom can be used to cure people who were bitten.

### Antivenom is hard to find

Unfortunately, it's hard to make antivenom. So it can be hard to get antivenom. As a result, many people in India are working hard to gather venom. These people have courage. They catch cobras or vipers. Then, they get the snake to bite through a piece of plastic into a container. The venom goes into the container. Then, the venom can be made into antivenom.

A snake gets milked for its venom.

CCS: RI.3.10

**Saving snakes**

Because there are some dangerous snakes in India, many people try to kill any snakes they find. People often kill snakes they find in their homes or on their farms. This is a problem because snakes are helpful in India. They eat mice and rats. Mice and rats are little thieves and eat people's food. Also, sometimes people kill snakes that aren't dangerous. And people get bitten when they try to kill dangerous snakes.

Because so many snakes have been killed, there are fewer snakes in India. As a result, many people around India are trying to help snakes. They are teaching people how to tell the difference between regular snakes and dangerous snakes. They are also gathering antivenom. Also, if a family finds a dangerous snake in their home, they can now call people to help. These people will come and take the dangerous snake away safely. They'll bring the snake back to the wild, where it can live in nature.

**TIP 2: Compare and contrast information in two different texts.**

Both "The Truth About Snakes" and "Snake Champions" contain facts about snakes. You can compare and contrast the facts. To **compare** means to find facts that are alike. To **contrast** means to find facts that are different. A **Venn diagram** is a graphic organizer that you can use to compare and contrast two things.

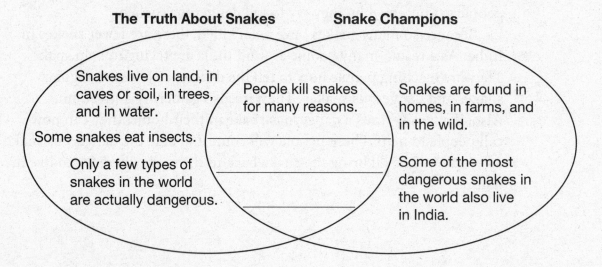

**The Truth About Snakes**     **Snake Champions**

Snakes live on land, in caves or soil, in trees, and in water.

Some snakes eat insects.

Only a few types of snakes in the world are actually dangerous.

People kill snakes for many reasons.

Snakes are found in homes, in farms, and in the wild.

Some of the most dangerous snakes in the world also live in India.

3. The facts in the Venn diagram are from the two texts. Reread "The Truth About Snakes" and "Snake Champions." Underline the facts shown in the Venn diagram when you find them in the texts.

4. Look for more facts that are found in both texts. Write a fact in the shared space in the Venn diagram.

CCS: L.3.6

 **TIP 3: Look for words that describe location, or space.**

When reading nonfiction (or true stories), you can learn a lot by paying attention to words that describe location, or space. Words that describe space tell you about where things are or are going, and they sometimes compare the locations of things.

You are probably familiar with many of these words that describe space.

| | |
|---|---|
| left | right |
| under | over |
| around | through |
| there | here |
| into | in |

 **Practice Activity 1**

**Directions:** Look back at "The Truth About Snakes." Then answer the following questions.

1. This sentence from the passage includes a word that describes space.

   "Still others live in rivers, swamps, or oceans."

   Underline the word that describes space.

2. Describe how the word tells you about where snakes live.

   _____

   _____

   _____

3. Find words that describe space in "The Truth About Snakes." Circle these words in the text.

**TIP 4: Use transition words to understand a true story.**

In most stories or articles, events happen in order, one after another. When you read a passage, you'll often see words that will help you follow the order in which actions take place. These words may also tell you about how actions are connected.

Here are some words to look for:

| | | | | |
|---|---|---|---|---|
| first | before | following | now | as a result |
| next | after | at last | later | because |
| last | at first | then | while | as soon as |

Read these sentences from "Snake Champions."

> First, a scientist needs venom from an actual snake. Then, the scientist uses the venom to make antivenom. The scientist changes the venom into medicine. Finally, the antivenom can be used to cure people who were bitten.

5. Circle transition words in these sentences.

6. Think about the order of the actions described in these sentences. What action happens after a scientist makes antivenom?

_____

7. What action happens before a scientist makes antivenom?

_____

 **Practice Activity 2**

**Directions:** Complete the following sentences using the list of transition words.

1. Martin washed his hands _____ they were dirty.

2. We cleaned the whole house _____ my grandmother came to visit.

3. _____ of all the hours spent practicing, our team won the game!

CCS: RL.3.4

 **TIP 5:  Look for literal and figurative language.**

In Lesson 8, you learned about how a writer uses literal and figurative language in fiction. You learned that **literal language** is when the writer clearly means exactly what is written. **Figurative language**, such as similes and metaphors, suggests extra meaning. Nonfiction writers also use literal and figurative language in their writing. Sound devices, such as repeating consonant sounds and using sensory details (sight, smell, touch, hearing, taste), help the reader remember an important point that the writer makes.

8.  Find an example of a simile in "The Truth About Snakes."

    _____

9.  Find an example of a metaphor in "Snake Champions."

    _____

10. Locate two sensory details in "The Truth About Snakes" and "Snake Champions." Write each example below and tell why the author used the sensory detail.

    Sensory detail from "The Truth About Snakes": _____

    _____

    _____

    Sensory detail from "Snake Champions": _____

    _____

    _____

**TIP 6:** **Use the text to find information.**

When reading nonfiction, you can use special text to find information. You can use bold words, key words, headings, and pictures or diagrams to help you find information.

**bold words** — Bold words are **darker**. You can spot a **bold** word easily.

**key words** — Key words are clues that help you find information. Writers usually include a lot of key words when describing a new or complicated idea.

**headings** — Headings are small titles for different parts of a nonfiction passage. In the passage "The Truth About Snakes," there are four headings.

**pictures** or **diagrams** — Pictures and diagrams show what the writer is describing in the text. They can have captions (words that describe the picture). Look at the picture of the snake on page 102.

When reading nonfiction online, you can use the tools above. You can also use sidebars and hyperlinks to help you find information.

**sidebars** — Sidebars are words or sentences that are placed to the left or right side of the main text. A webpage has a main passage in the center, but it can also have sidebars to the sides. Print pages can also have sidebars, too. Sidebars list key details or extra passages related to the main passage.

**hyperlinks** — A hyperlink is a word or phrase on a webpage that can be clicked to bring you to another webpage.

11. Write the four headings in "The Truth About Snakes."

_____

_____

_____

_____

**Lesson Practice begins on the following page.**

**Directions:** This passage is about sneezing. Read the passage. Then answer Numbers 1 through 5.

# To Sneeze or Not to Sneeze?

by Janet Morimoto

Take a deep breath and imagine that it's springtime. The sun is shining, and flowers are blooming. Every breeze is filled with pollen, a yellow dust that plants make. Suddenly, there is a little tickle deep in your nose. Watch out! You are about to sneeze!

A sneeze can make your nose feel itchy.

### What causes a sneeze?

Grains of pollen can make people sneeze. A pet shedding fur can also make you sneeze. You may sneeze because you are getting sick. So when you get that little tickle and you feel one coming on, should you sneeze or not?

### What is a sneeze?

Let's look at a sneeze in slow motion. When a nose gets itchy from dust, pollen, or a cold, it needs help. The brain sends a special order to the nose, mouth, and chest to get rid of the itch. Then these parts of the body work together to suck in a large amount of air. The belly muscles tighten to help push the air out of the body. The eyes close just before the sneeze.

All of a sudden, *ah—ah-choo*! Spray travels from the nose and mouth at up to 100 miles per hour. That's faster than a pitch in a baseball game! Now imagine thousands of baseballs flying into the air at the same time. That's how many droplets of spray fly out during a sneeze. And that is why it's important to cover your nose and mouth every time you sneeze.

**What should you do about a sneeze?**

Sneezing creates a problem: it spreads germs. If you don't cover your nose and mouth, you may sneeze onto anyone who's near you. That is *not* a good thing! So when you feel a sneeze coming on, grab a tissue if one is handy. Then be sure you wash your hands right away. Better still, try to sneeze into the inside of your elbow. This is a good way to keep from spreading germs. It's polite to say "Excuse me" after you sneeze.

**Should you see a doctor?**

If you sneeze, should you see a doctor? If you sneeze only once or twice, you probably don't need to. If you keep sneezing and can't stop, then it might be good to get a checkup.

For example, when pollen in the air makes you sneeze, your body makes something called histamine. Histamine can make your eyes red and itchy. It can cause a runny nose. If you live in the country, you breathe in a lot of pollen, so your body makes more histamine. Medicines called antihistamines can help you feel better. Antihistamines can help you stop sneezing. But remember, you should check with a doctor before using them.

So, should you sneeze? Yes, go ahead and sneeze. It's okay to sneeze. Just be careful to cover your nose and mouth when you do. And if you can't stop sneezing, see a doctor. You should never try to force yourself to hold back a sneeze, because you might sneeze inside your head. This could hurt your ears and breathing passages. So please sneeze carefully!

1.  **Why did the author <u>most likely</u> write "To Sneeze or Not to Sneeze?"**

    A.  to give information about sneezing

    B.  to tell about the history of medicine

    C.  to get readers to cover their mouths

    D.  to entertain readers with a funny story

2.  **What happens when your body makes histamine?**

    A.  It stops you from sneezing.

    B.  It makes you breathe in pollen.

    C.  It helps you to feel better.

    D.  It makes your eyes red and itchy.

3.  **Which statement about sneezes is <u>most</u> important to the main idea?**

    A.  "You may sneeze because you are getting sick."

    B.  "That's faster than a pitch in a baseball game!"

    C.  "Antihistamines can help you stop sneezing."

    D.  "Yes, go ahead and sneeze."

4.  **In what section of the article can you find information about using a tissue?**

    A.  What causes a sneeze?

    B.  What is a sneeze?

    C.  What should you do about a sneeze?

    D.  Should you see a doctor?

5.   Look back at the article "To Sneeze or Not to Sneeze." Compare and contrast the facts in these sections: "What Causes a Sneeze?" and "Should You See a Doctor?" Find facts that are different and find facts that are similar. Use these facts to fill in the Venn diagram below.

**What Causes a Sneeze?**      **Should You See A Doctor?**

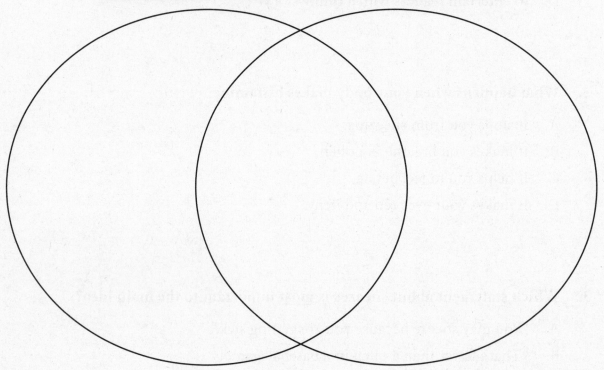

CCSs: RL.3.10, RI.3.9

# Lesson 11: Making Connections

"Until 1969, no one had ever touched the moon. No one!" growled Max in a low voice. "Then the astronauts of *Apollo 11* landed."

"What are you talking about, *weirdo*?" asked Jessica with a giggle.

"You must not have read *Man on the Moon* by Anastasia Suen," Max said matter-of-factly. "It's only the most awesome storybook on Earth. It tells about the first landing on the moon."

"Well, for your information, Mr. Smarty-pants, my parents have a videotape of the real thing! But I'll trade you my video for your book, if you think you could be without it for a day!"

The same story can be told in many different ways. The writer of *Man on the Moon* told about the first landing differently from other writers. Television programs, movies, and news articles all told the story of the landing in different ways.

Every kind of writer makes choices about what to include, what to leave out, and what to tell as very important. For example, the writer of *Man on the Moon* chose to leave out a lot of space program history. Instead she wrote mostly about the moon-landing mission. She wanted her readers to feel as though they had traveled to the moon with the astronauts. Her choices about what to put in the book (and what to leave out) affected the story she told.

CCSs: RL.3.10, RI.3.9

Read two accounts about the first landing on the moon. Look carefully to see how they are alike and different. The first account is written as a drama (play). The scene shows the action that took place on July 20, 1969, when Neil Armstrong and Edwin "Buzz" Aldrin became the first humans to walk on the moon.

from

# *Moon Landing*

by Jill Foley

*(Two astronauts in spacesuits sit at the controls of the* Eagle, *a small landing craft. They are preparing to land on the surface of the moon. A soft, yellow light beams through the window of the spacecraft. In the background, radio voices and buzzings are heard.)*

**NEIL:** *(into his headset)* Houston . . . the *Eagle* has landed.

**HOUSTON:** Roger, Neil. We copy. The *Eagle* has landed.

**BUZZ:** That was a smooth landing, Neil, and just in time. Our fuel is almost gone.

**NEIL:** We've done it. We've landed on the moon. Just look at it!

**BUZZ:** I could rest for a few minutes, but if we want to get our moonwalk done today, we'd better get ready. There are probably lots of people waiting for us to step out of the *Eagle* and onto the moon.

**NEIL:** No one is more ready than I am.

**BUZZ:** Except for me!

*(The men struggle into their backpack units and prepare to open the door of their spaceship. They look at each other silently and then open the door. NEIL steps out onto the powdery surface.)*

**NEIL:** That's one small step for man, one giant leap for mankind.

*(NEIL looks back to BUZZ. They exchange "thumbs-up" signals.)*

Here is an article written about the same moon landing for the following day's newspaper.

---

SPACE CENTER, Houston—A little after 4:00 p.m. Sunday, mankind reached the powdery surface of the moon.

Neil Armstrong and Edwin "Buzz" Aldrin Jr. made a perfect landing. It was so good, in fact, that NASA allowed the men to go ahead with their moonwalk Sunday night instead of waiting until Monday morning.

Several hours after landing, at 10:56 p.m., Armstrong stepped from the *Eagle* to the moon's surface.

"That's one small step for man, one giant leap for mankind," he said as he touched the cold surface of the moon.

"I can see my footprints in the fine particles. There seems to be no difficulty in moving around," Armstrong told Mission Control as he tested man's ability to walk on the moon for the first time.

---

 **TIP 1: Compare details within the passages.**

When you're asked to compare two passages, first see whether both give the same details. In this case, both passages tell about the first trip to the moon. But each passage was written from a different point of view, so the details are not the same.

1. Different authors tell the same facts with different words. Find two details that are given in both passages and underline them.

2. Which of the following events takes place in both the drama and the newspaper article?

   A. Buzz Aldrin says, "That was a smooth touchdown, Neil."

   B. Neil Armstrong says, "I can see my footprints in the fine particles."

   C. Neil Armstrong says, "We've done it. We've landed on the moon. Just look at it!"

   D. Neil Armstrong says, "That's one small step for man, one giant leap for mankind."

3. When your teacher instructs you to do so, discuss with your classmates how the passages are different.

**TIP 2:  See if one passage can help you to understand the other.**

Sometimes the details in one passage will help you to better understand another passage. Notice how the drama gives you a better sense of the astronauts' feelings than the newspaper article does.

4.  List some ways the newspaper article helps you understand the drama.

_____

_____

 **TIP 3:  Tell the difference between your point of view and the point of view of the characters in the story.**

In Lesson 6, you learned about point of view and how your point of view is often different from the point of view of the characters in a story or the writer of the story. Point of view describes the way that a character sees or thinks about something. It is the opinion and feelings the character has toward something.

In the play "Moon Landing" on page 114, Neil, Houston, and Buzz have different points of view.

5.  When they land on the moon, Buzz says, "That was a smooth landing, Neil, and just in time. Our fuel is almost gone." How does Buzz probably think or feel about the landing?

_____

_____

6.  When they land on the moon, Neil says, "We've done it. We've landed on the moon. Just look at it!" How does Neil probably think or feel about the landing?

_____

_____

7.  When you read "Moon Landing," how did you feel about the landing?

_____

_____

CCSs: RI.3.6, RI.3.10

 **TIP 4: Compare and contrast your point of view with the author's point of view.**

In Lesson 6, you learned that point of view describes the way that someone sees or thinks about something. It is the opinion and feelings the person has toward something. You can describe your own point of view as well as the point of view of the author.

When you read a text, you may start out with an opinion about the topic. Your opinion may change. You may agree or disagree with the author's opinion or point of view.

Read "Food in Space."

## *Food in Space*

You may have heard about astronaut ice cream. It's a treat that tastes like ice cream but is dry and crumbly. Most foods astronauts eat have to be different. It's hard for them to eat anything that can be messy in space. Most of the foods are dried. Then they add water. Sometimes they sip them through big straws, like chicken soup or mushroom soup. They even eat stew and scrambled eggs this way! There are some foods astronauts get to use forks and knives with, like macaroni and cheese and chicken and rice. Astronauts have a lot of food with them in space. There's always more than enough food, so astronauts don't have to worry about what's for dinner!

8. What do you know about what astronauts eat in space? Write any thoughts, opinions, and feelings about this topic.

_____

_____

_____

9. What is your overall opinion or feeling about this topic? This is your point of view.

_____

_____

10. What do you know about the author's overall opinions or feelings about what astronauts eat in space? Write the author's point of view.

_____

_____

11. Now, look back at your point of view and the author's point of view. How are they alike or different?

_____

_____

**TIP 5: Compare and contrast parts of different stories.**

There are times when you may read different stories written about the same people or characters. You may also read different stories written by the same author. You can compare and contrast the plots, settings, themes, and characters in different stories. You can notice things that are alike or different.

Read the descriptions of three different books in a series:

*The Berenstain Bears Visit the Dentist:* Sister Bear has a loose tooth, and Brother Bear needs a checkup. So they all go to the dentist. Sister Bear is scared, but then she learns the dentist is nice and helpful.

*The Berenstain Bears and Too Much Junk Food:* Sister Bear, Brother Bear, and Papa Bear eat too much junk food. Their doctor teaches them about the right foods to eat, and they learn to eat healthier.

*The Berenstain Bears and Too Much Teasing:* Brother Bear teases Sister Bear, which makes her sad. Then at school, a bully teases Brother Bear. He learns a lesson about how teasing can hurt, and he stops teasing Sister Bear.

12. What is the same about the stories? _____

_____

13. What is different about the stories? _____

_____

CCSs: L.3.5b, L.3.5c

 **TIP 6:  Connect the words in a story to your life.**

Writers pick certain words to use in their stories. They want you to read the words and connect the words to your own life. To make connections to words, you can think about times from your life when the word was used.

14.  Look at the words below. For each one, think of someone or something in your life that fits the word.

friendly

helpful

curious

15.  In *The Berenstain Bears Visit the Dentist*, Sister Bear is scared of the dentist but later learns that the dentist is nice and helpful. Think of someone in your life who was scared of something at first and then learned not to be scared.

 **TIP 7:  Understand related words with similar meanings.**

To make connections to words, you can also think about how some words are related and have similar meanings.

16.  For each word in the chart, think of words with similar meanings. Write as many other words as you can think of that share similar meanings. The first one has been done for you.

| Word | Words with Similar Meanings |
|------|------------------------------|
| Know | think, wonder, learn, believe |
| Feel |  |
| Say |  |

**Practice Activity**

**Directions:** Read both sentences for each question. Then identify the correct answer.

1. Hot Dog was the best dog the cops at the precinct ever had!
   Judge Rat peered through his glasses at the thieves in front of him.

   How are the characters different?

   A. Hot Dog is a cop, and Judge Rat is a judge.

   B. Hot Dog is a dog, and Judge Rat is a rat.

   C. Hot Dog is a dog, and Judge Rat is a judge.

   D. Hot Dog is a cop, and Judge Rat is a thief.

2. Al gathered tree leaves for his science project while hiking through the forest.

   The mountain gorilla lives in the forests of central Africa.

   How are the settings alike?

   A. Both settings are in Africa.

   B. Both settings are in science class.

   C. Both settings are in Al's home.

   D. Both settings are in a forest.

3. Lisa couldn't find her favorite paintbrush, so she looked everywhere.
   Marco needed to paint his grandmother's apartment, so he asked his friends to help.

   How are the plots different?

   A. Lisa is trying to solve her problem on her own, but Marco asks his friends to help him solve his problem.

   B. Lisa knows that she needs a paintbrush, but Marco doesn't know that he needs a paintbrush.

   C. Lisa knows how to paint, but Marco doesn't know how to paint.

   D. Lisa has a problem, but Marco doesn't have a problem.

**Lesson Practice begins on the following page.**

**Directions:** These passages are folktales. They are both similar to the story "Cinderella." Read the passages. Then answer Numbers 1 through 10.

# *Turkey Girl*

### a folktale of the Zuni Indians retold by Red Gomez

Turkey Girl lived in a farming village with two mean stepsisters. They were called Yellow Corn and Blue Corn. They made Turkey Girl do all the chores. She even had to take care of all the village turkeys.

Now, every year there was a festival called the Corn Dance. Turkey Girl wanted to go to the Corn Dance, but her stepsisters would not let her. "What would you wear?" they asked. "You have only rags for clothes. Stay with your friends, the turkeys. We will go to the dance instead and dance with the bravest warriors."

Poor Turkey Girl was sad. She took her flock of turkeys out to a patch of wild grain and sang them the saddest songs.

They took pity on poor Turkey Girl. "We will make clothes for you to go to the dance," they said. So, they made Turkey Girl a beautiful robe, soft moccasins, and a belt of feathers. "Go to the dance, but be back by sundown to take us to shelter," the turkeys said. "That's when the coyotes come out, looking for dinner."

Turkey Girl had to take care of the village turkeys.

Turkey Girl went to the Corn Dance and was so happy. The bravest warriors waited in line to dance with her. Turkey Girl was so proud. She could see that her stepsisters were angry and jealous.

The hour came when the sun set behind the mountains. Turkey Girl was still dancing. Suddenly, Turkey Girl remembered. She hurried back to her flock. "Oh, my turkeys," she cried, "I have let you down."

When she returned to the patch of grain, the turkeys were gone.

"Turkey Girl has forgotten about us," they had cried. Then they flew off in every direction to escape the hungry coyotes.

Remember this, children. Don't be like Turkey Girl! Just because you're having a good time, don't forget those who have helped you or those who depend on you.

# Maha and the Little Red Fish

a folktale from Iraq retold by Marsha Pruitt

Near the sea, a little girl named Maha once lived with her father, her stepmother, and her stepsister. When her father was at home, the stepmother spoke to Maha with a voice as sweet as honey. But when he went to the sea to fish each day, the woman made Maha do all of the chores.

One day, Maha spotted a small red fish among those she was cleaning for supper. "Please return me to the sea, for I am a magic fish," said the little red fish. "I will grant you anything you wish, for kindness never goes unrewarded."

Maha removed the little fish from her net and gently returned it to the sea.

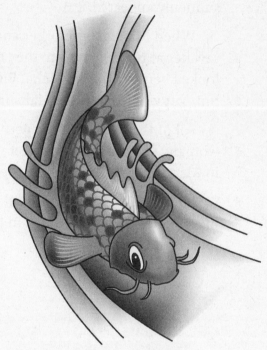

Maha released the magic fish.

The years went by, and Maha and her stepsister grew to be young women. Maha worked from sunrise to sunset, but every day she became kinder and more beautiful.

One day, the daughter of an important man was to be married. Maha wished she could go to sing and dance and watch the bride as her hands and feet were decorated with red henna stain. But instead, the stepmother made Maha help get her stepsister prepared for the celebration.

> **henna** = a reddish brown dye

The day of the wedding, Maha went to the sea's edge to seek the advice of the little red fish. "Little fish, what should I do? Will I be my stepmother's servant forever?" asked Maha. "I wish to go to the bride's henna like all of the other girls."

"You shall go," said the little red fish. "And you shall even sit next to the bride."

On the grass nearby, a silken gown, a pearl comb, and some clogs made out of gold suddenly appeared.

> **bride's henna** = a party during which a bride is decorated with henna for her wedding

When Maha's stepmother and stepsister saw her at the celebration, they thought she looked very much like Maha. But then they laughed and thought how funny it would be to see Maha in such nice clothes.

All of the women at the party thought that Maha was a nice young woman. The mother of a sweet young man named Abdul saw the kindness in Maha's eyes. "You shall be the perfect bride for my son!" she exclaimed.

Soon after, Maha and Abdul were wed right near the sea, where Maha's little red fish could take part in the ceremony. Maha lived happily from that day on.

1. Which of the following pairs of characters from <u>both</u> stories are <u>most alike</u>?

   A. the coyotes and Maha's stepmother

   B. Turkey Girl's stepsisters and Maha

   C. Turkey Girl and Maha's stepsister

   D. the turkeys and the little red fish

2. Which of the following does <u>not</u> apply to "Turkey Girl" and "Maha and the Little Red Fish"?

   A. Both have happy endings.

   B. Both are about a young woman.

   C. Both are very old folktales.

   D. Both tell about magical animals.

3. Which event in the second passage is <u>similar</u> to Turkey Girl going to the Corn Dance in the first passage?

   A. Maha's stepmother acting sweet as honey

   B. Maha finding a little red fish

   C. Maha going to the bride's henna

   D. Maha cleaning fish for supper

4. Which of the following happens in <u>both</u> passages?

   A. Magical animals help the main character.

   B. A Corn Dance makes the main character forget her duty.

   C. An evil stepmother makes the main character work.

   D. A handsome prince rescues the main character.

5.  Which event in "Turkey Girl" is like the appearance of the silken gown, pearl comb, and gold clogs in "Maha and the Little Red Fish"?

    A.  Turkey Girl takes her flock to a patch of wild grain.

    B.  Turkey Girl's stepsisters tell her she has only rags for clothes.

    C.  Brave warriors stand in line to dance with Turkey Girl.

    D.  The turkeys make Turkey Girl beautiful clothes for the Corn Dance.

6.  Which of the following best contrasts Maha and Turkey Girl?

    A.  Turkey Girl had only one mean stepsister. Maha had two mean stepsisters.

    B.  Maha had a very happy home life. Turkey Girl had a very unhappy home life.

    C.  Maha had a good time at the henna. Turkey Girl had a bad time at the Corn Dance.

    D.  Maha took good care of the animal that helped her. Turkey Girl forgot about the animals that helped her.

7.  Which of the following best describes the point of view of the turkeys at the end of "Turkey Girl"?

    A.  They were angry and jealous of Turkey Girl dancing with the bravest warriors.

    B.  They were upset that Turkey Girl forgot about them, and they were scared of coyotes.

    C.  They were happy that Turkey Girl remembered them while she was dancing.

    D.  They felt pity for Turkey Girl and wanted her to stay at the dance.

8.  Which of the following best describes the point of view of Abdul's mother in "Maha and the Little Red Fish"?

    A.  She thought she looked a lot like the bride.

    B.  She saw kindness in Maha's eyes.

    C.  She laughed when she saw Maha in nice clothes.

    D.  She didn't want Maha to go to the bride's henna.

9. Describe <u>two</u> ways that Turkey Girl and Maha are <u>alike</u>. Explain your answer with two details from the story.

1. _____

_____

_____

_____

2. _____

_____

_____

_____

10. List one way that reading "Turkey Girl" helped you understand "Maha and the Little Red Fish."

_____

_____

_____

_____

CCSs: RL.3.7, RI.3.7, RI.3.10

# Lesson 12: Reading Pictures

Did you ever hear the saying "A picture is worth a thousand words"? This means that one picture or photograph can tell a story better than words. It's always a good idea to look at pictures and drawings *before* you begin reading. The pictures and drawings give you information about the setting, characters, and plot in the story.

This lesson will help you use pictures, drawings, and graphics to find information.

 **TIP 1: Pictures explain or describe information.**

Pictures give more information about the ideas in a passage. Look at this picture. It tells you about the setting, the character, and the plot of a story.

1.  What does the picture say about the setting, character, and plot?

    _____

    _____

    _____

    _____

    _____

    _____

CCSs: RI.3.7, RI.3.10

 **TIP 2:  Picture graphs show information with pictures.**

**Picture graphs** (sometimes called **pictographs**) use pictures to show information. If a picture graph tells the number of ice cream cones sold each day of the week, it may use pictures of ice cream cones. For example, this picture might stand for one ice cream cone sold, or it might stand for 10 ice cream cones sold. You must look at the graph's **key** to find out what each picture stands for.

**Example:**

Use the picture graph that follows to answer Numbers 2 and 3.

Here is a picture graph that shows the number of boys and girls in Mrs. Smith's third-grade class. Look at the key before you answer the questions.

**Boys and Girls in Mrs. Smith's Third-Grade Class**

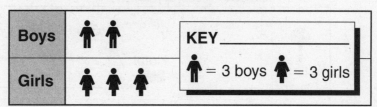

2.  How many boys are in Mrs. Smith's third-grade class?

   A.  two

   B.  three

   C.  five

   D.  six

3.  How many girls are in Mrs. Smith's third-grade class?

   A.  three

   B.  six

   C.  nine

   D.  twelve

**TIP 3: Maps are small drawings of large areas.**

Model airplanes are designed to be small copies of full-size airplanes. Like models, **maps** are small copies, but they represent full-size areas of land.

Maps use a drawing called a **compass** to show north, south, east, and west. They also use a line called a **scale** to measure the distance between things. Maps can show rivers, roads, lakes, towns, airports, buildings, and so on.

Maps, like picture graphs, have a key. Always look at a map's key so that you know what each picture on the map stands for.

Maps usually have letters along one side and numbers along the top or the bottom. These numbers and letters can be used like the labels on a chart. For example, Blue Lake's water tower is located at A-1.

Now study the Blue Lake map and key. Then answer Numbers 4 through 8.

**Map of Blue Lake**

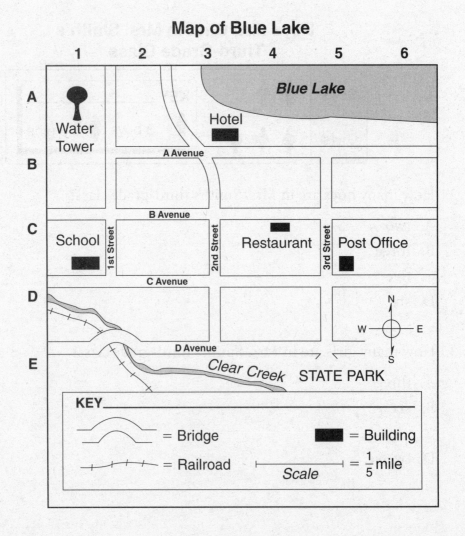

4. Clear Creek runs under the

   A. A Avenue bridge.

   B. B Avenue bridge.

   C. C Avenue bridge.

   D. D Avenue bridge.

5. If you walked from the Blue Lake Restaurant to the post office, which street would you have to cross?

   A. A Avenue

   B. 3rd Street

   C. 2nd Street

   D. 1st Street

6. Blue Lake School is located at the corner of

   A. A Avenue and 1st Street.

   B. B Avenue and 2nd Street.

   C. C Avenue and 1st Street.

   D. D Avenue and 3rd Street.

7. Which of the following is located at C-4?

   A. a hotel

   B. a school

   C. a restaurant

   D. a water tower

8. If you walked from Blue Lake School to the post office, in which direction would you be going?

   A. east

   B. west

   C. north

   D. south

**TIP 4: Recipes are a type of list with steps.**

A **recipe** gives you step-by-step instructions on how to prepare food. It is important to read a recipe all the way through before you begin to cook. By doing this, you will know what you need. Sometimes recipes include a picture of what the final dish should look like.

Most recipes begin with a list of ingredients and tools. Ingredients are the food items that you will need. After you have gathered all of the food items needed, look at what else you will need. You may need forks, spoons, mixing bowls, and so on. These will help you to combine your ingredients.

Once you have read through the instructions and gathered everything you need, you are ready to get cooking. Follow the instructions carefully. If you miss a step, you could ruin the meal! Below is a recipe that is simple but delicious.

 **Practice Activity**

**Directions:** Read the recipe, then answer Numbers 1 through 5.

### Lemonade

**What you need:**

1 eight-ounce drinking glass

2 tablespoons lemon juice

2 tablespoons sugar

   cold water

   ice cubes

**What you do:**

1. Using the measuring spoon, put two tablespoons of lemon juice into a glass.

2. Put two tablespoons of sugar into the glass.

3. Add water and ice cubes. Then stir with a teaspoon.

1. Which of the following items is not needed for making lemonade?

  A. lemon juice

  B. sugar

  C. ice

  D. measuring cup

2. Which of the following items is needed for making lemonade but is not listed?

   A. teaspoon

   B. flour

   C. salt

   D. ice cubes

3. What is the first thing you should do when making lemonade?

   A. Add two tablespoons of sugar.

   B. Add water and ice cubes.

   C. Stir the lemonade.

   D. Add two tablespoons of juice.

4. Which of these steps comes last in the instructions?

   A. Stir.

   B. Add 2 tablespoons of sugar.

   C. Add water.

   D. Add ice cubes.

5. If you skipped Step 2, your lemonade would be

   A. too sweet.

   B. too sour.

   C. too cold.

   D. too warm.

**Lesson Practice begins on the following page.**

**Directions:** This passage is about the St. Louis Zoo. Read the passage and look at the map. Then answer Numbers 1 through 8.

# A Trip to the Zoo

### by Cathy Rossi

St. Louis has one of the best zoos in the country. The zoo keeps changing. If you haven't been to the St. Louis Zoo lately, you might have missed something. Let's take a tour.

River's Edge shows what river waters are like in Missouri and around the world. Follow the river path to learn about local wetlands and waters. See how animals use rivers in places like Africa, Asia, and South America. Watch hippos sink underwater, rhinos play in mud, and elephants clean themselves. It's an exciting journey.

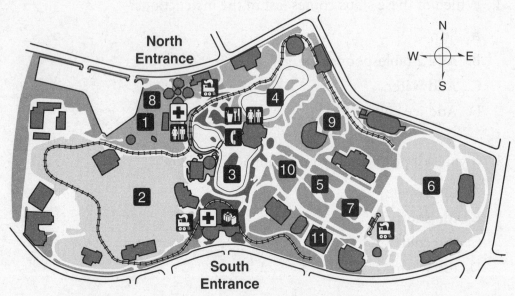

**KEY**

| | | |
|---|---|---|
| **1** Discovery Corner | **7** Bird House | 🍴 Food |
| **2** River's Edge | **8** Children's Zoo | 🚻 Bathroom |
| **3** Lakeside Crossing | **9** Fragile Forest | 🎁 Gifts |
| **4** The Wild | **10** Sea Lion Arena | ✚ First Aid |
| **5** Historic Hill | **11** Primate House | ☎ Telephone |
| **6** Red Rocks | 🚂 Train Stop | |

At Historic Hill, you can view animals that fly, swim, and swing from trees. First, go to the Bird House to see birds of all colors and sizes. At the Sea Lion Arena, sea lions show off for crowds of people. Or, maybe you'd rather hang out at the Primate House and see how monkeys live.

In the Wild, some animals like cold weather, and others like it hot. You'll see polar bears, penguins, and other animals from icy parts of the world. You'll also see animals that live in steamy rain forests, where it is warm all year. Then, you'll enter a forest filled with apes, chimps, and gorillas. It is called the Fragile Forest because such forests are in danger of disappearing.

Discovery Corner is where you get to see how bugs live. You'll see butterflies in their flowery world. In the Children's Zoo, you can pet horses, goats, and rabbits. Discovery Corner also has a place called the Living World. It is a good place for you to learn more about the creatures that you'll see.

The last part of the zoo is called Red Rocks. You'll feel like you're in the wild, but you will be safe in the zoo. You can see lions and tigers in the areas where they live. Nearby, there are striped zebras and spotted giraffes. All of these animals need big spaces so they can move around and get exercise.

While roaming through the zoo, you'll get plenty of exercise, too. If you get tired, you can take the train from one part of the zoo to another. If you get hungry, there are plenty of places to stop for snacks and meals. You can spend a whole day enjoying the St. Louis Zoo. You will have fun, and you will learn about the world in which you live.

1.  **If you walked from Red Rocks to River's Edge, which direction would you be going?**

    A.  north

    B.  south

    C.  east

    D.  west

2.  **Where can you see butterflies?**

    A.  Discovery Corner

    B.  Lakeside Crossing

    C.  Red Rocks

    D.  Children's Zoo

3.  **Which of the following is not listed on the key?**

    A.  the Living World

    B.  the Children's Zoo

    C.  Sea Lion Arena

    D.  Primate House

4.  **Which animal can you find at number 4?**

    A.  hippos

    B.  rabbits

    C.  tigers

    D.  penguins

5.  **What is directly north of Lakeside Crossing?**

    A.  Gifts

    B.  First Aid

    C.  Telephone

    D.  Train

6.  **Which of the following happens in both River's Edge and Historic Hill?**

    A.  Animals swing from trees.

    B.  Animals are in the water.

    C.  Animals show off for crowds.

    D.  Animals play in the mud.

7.  **How do the pictures in "A Trip to the Zoo" help you understand the passage? Give two examples.**

    1. _____

    _____

    2. _____

    _____

8.  **Imagine you are at the Red Rocks area of the zoo. A friend of yours is coming through the North Entrance to meet you. You need to give directions to your friend to find you at the Red Rocks area. Write directions using details from the map and the passage.**

    _____

    _____

    _____

    _____

    _____

*Writing is no refuge... crystallizes thought and thought produces... Words are a lens to focus one's mind. Words are... something until I read what I've written.*

# Writing

Writers always have a **purpose**, or reason, for writing. You can figure out your purpose for writing before you write. Doing so will help you be a better writer.

You might write to:

- give information to a reader, such as with articles or letters.

- persuade a reader, such as with ads or editorials.

- teach a reader something, such as with how-to guidelines or manuals.

- entertain a reader, such as with stories or poems.

In this unit, you'll learn how to figure out your purpose and use your purpose to write well. Once you know your purpose, you can use this to help you do research, write a first draft, and revise your draft. If you practice using these tools, you will become a better writer.

## In This Unit

CCSs: W.3.7, W.3.8, W.3.10

# Lesson 13: Ready to Research

When you are planning to write, you should research. **Research** is the act of finding the information you need to use in your writing. You can research using encyclopedias, dictionaries, magazine articles, newspapers, books, the Internet, and other sources.

Research makes a piece of writing stronger. As a reader, you know that you rely on writing that contains facts and real information every day, such as bus schedules, recipes, and directions. As a writer, you need to make sure that what you write is supported by research.

 **TIP 1: Use many trusted sources when you research.**

When you research, you should use many sources. A **source** is where information comes from. You want to make sure to use trusted sources that you know contain facts and reliable information. By doing research with many trusted sources, you can be sure to support your ideas with facts and details.

## *More Sources!*

"I'm writing about our local swimming pool. I'm writing an article about how the water turned into grape jelly last Saturday afternoon," said Bryan. "My friend told me this happened, and I read it on a blog on the Internet."

Freda giggled. Freda was writing an article about how to swim the doggie paddle. She had

Freda did not find the pool to be grape jelly last Saturday. Although, it would have been a tasty adventure!

researched in an encyclopedia, read a magazine about swimming, and interviewed a swimming teacher. Freda had also been at the pool last Saturday afternoon, and the water had *not* been grape jelly!

"I think you should find some other trusted sources," Freda said, smiling. "Why don't you find some newspaper articles about the pool and ask the manager of the pool? You definitely need more sources and better sources to get the real information!"

CCSs: W.3.7, W.3.8, W.3.10

## Practice Activity 1

**Directions:** Look at the following sources. Circle the sources that you can trust.

| | | |
|---|---|---|
| a dictionary | something a stranger says | a scientific study |
| something written on a locker door | a newspaper article | an encyclopedia |
| a survey | a nonfiction book | a text message |

 **TIP 2: Be aware of your purpose for writing.**

A **purpose** is the reason why you are writing. Knowing your purpose is helpful when choosing what to write and how to write about it. Your purpose for writing an essay might be to do a report for school, report on something for the school newspaper, or prove someone wrong. There are other purposes, as well.

1. You decide to write step-by-step instructions on how to make a balloon animal. What would be your purpose in writing this?

_____

 **TIP 3: Ask yourself questions about the information you need.**

Before you begin to look for information, decide what kinds of questions you want to answer. This will make your research easier.

For example, imagine you wanted to write about dinosaurs. You might ask yourself, *When did dinosaurs live?* or *How big was the biggest dinosaur?* or *Were there any dinosaurs that ate other dinosaurs?*

 **TIP 4: Use an encyclopedia to learn a little bit about almost anything.**

Often, an encyclopedia will be the information source you turn to. An **encyclopedia** is a book that gives information about all types of topics. You can use an encyclopedia to find out about famous people, places, animals, things, and even events in history. An encyclopedia has articles on many topics. **Articles** are reports that give information on specific topics. The articles in encyclopedias are in alphabetical order, by topic.

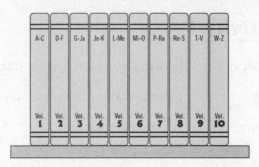

2. In which volume of the encyclopedias above would you find information about dinosaurs?

A. Volume 2

C. Volume 4

B. Volume 3

D. Volume 5

 **TIP 5: Magazines and newspapers contain many kinds of information.**

**Magazines** have articles about many kinds of things. Some magazines, such as *Time* and *Newsweek*, have articles about what's happening in the world. Other magazines have articles about hobbies, cooking, music, or sports. Many magazines have made-up stories and true stories.

Some magazines are written just for kids. Examples are *Cricket* and *Highlights for Children*. Can you think of others? If so, list their titles on the lines below.

3. _____

_____

_____

**Newspapers** tell about important day-to-day events. A newspaper may tell about events across the world or in your hometown. What is the name of a newspaper in your hometown?

4. _____

Most newspapers are printed every day. Newspapers give more up-to-date information than magazines. They usually give more information about a subject than a television or radio news program, although news sites on the Internet, TV, and radio stations provide the most up-to-date news.

CCSs: W.3.7, W.3.8, W.3.10

 **TIP 6:  You can look for information in many other sources.**

When you are researching, you are not limited to encyclopedias, newspapers, and magazines. You can find information anywhere!

Different sources give you different information.

- To find out what a word means or how to say it, look in a **dictionary**.

- To find out what other words mean the same as the word you're using, look in a **thesaurus**.

- To find information on a map, such as where a city is located or how far away it is, look at an **atlas**.

- To find out what something looks like, look at pictures or photographs.

- To find out what something looks like in action, look at a video or television program.

Now answer Numbers 5 through 7.

5. Which source would most likely tell you about what happened in the United States yesterday?

   A. a dictionary          C. a daily newspaper

   B. an encyclopedia       D. a magazine

6. Where would you look to find another word for *excited*?

   A. a dictionary          C. an atlas

   B. a thesaurus           D. an encyclopedia

7. Which source would best tell you how far it is from Allendale to Columbia?

   A. an atlas              C.  an encyclopedia

   B. a newspaper           D.  a dictionary

**TIP 7: Use libraries and talk to people when looking for information.**

Don't forget about asking people for information. Parents, teachers, or someone who knows about your topic can help you. People who work in your library can be extra helpful. They can help you find information of all kinds.

Another thing you can find in most school and public libraries is a connection to the Internet. The **Internet** is an electronic tool that helps you find nearly any kind of information. You can use a computer to view pages of information. These **Web pages** are like the pages of a book, except they are on a computer. Some libraries also have a collection of CDs and DVDs that cover many topics.

8. Which person could give you the best information about taking care of your dog's health?

   A. a dentist　　　　　　　C. a teacher

   B. a librarian　　　　　　D. an animal doctor

 **TIP 8: Judge a book by its cover.**

No, we don't mean you can tell whether a book is good just by looking at it. But you can tell a lot from the information that's on the cover, such as the title. The **title** is the name of the book. You can also tell a lot from the titles of magazine articles, Web sites, and so on.

For example, imagine your teacher asked you to write a report about northern cardinals, a common type of bird. You go to the library and find four books with the word *cardinal* in the title:

> *Baseball Teams: The St. Louis Cardinals*
>
> *Northern Cardinals*
>
> *Candy the Cardinal and Other Stories*
>
> *The Cardinal in Flight: Nature Poems*

Before you start paging through every one of these books looking for information about northern cardinals, you can probably decide to leave two of them on the shelf.

9. Which book most likely contains facts about cardinals you can use in your report?

CCSs: W.3.7, W.3.8, W.3.10

 **TIP 9:** **Use the table of contents.**

Now that you've found a book that matches the topic of your report (northern cardinals), it's time to find the information you need. You could read the whole book until you find what you want. Or, you could use the tools that the author put in the book to help you find what you need. The first tool is called the table of contents.

The **table of contents** is a list at the beginning of the book of the book's chapters. **Chapters** are parts of the book that are about different things. The table of contents lists the chapter titles and the number of each chapter's first page. By looking at the table of contents and reading the chapter titles, you can understand how the information in a book is organized.

Look at this table of contents from a book about northern cardinals. Use it to answer Numbers 10 through 13 on the next page.

---

### Northern Cardinals

### Table of Contents

| Chapter | Page |
|---|---|
| **1** How to Spot a Cardinal | 2 |
| **2** Where Cardinals Live | 21 |
| **3** What Cardinals Eat | 32 |
| **4** Cardinals' Nests | 41 |
| **5** Cardinals' Family Life | 57 |
| **6** How to Get Cardinals to Come to You | 71 |
| Glossary | 95 |

---

10. Which page would you turn to if you wanted to know what kind of food cardinals eat?

    A. 21

    B. 32

    C. 41

    D. 71

11. Which page would you turn to if you wanted to know where to find cardinals?

    A. 21

    B. 32

    C. 41

    D. 71

12. Which chapter describes what cardinals look like?

    A. 1

    B. 2

    C. 3

    D. 4

13. What is Chapter 4 about?

    _____

CCSs: W.3.7, W.3.8, W.3.10

 **TIP 10: Use the index.**

Another tool in many books is the index. An **index** lists every topic in the book. The list is in alphabetical order. This means that the first topics listed begin with *A*, then with *B*, and so on. The index has many more details than the table of contents. An index also gives you the page number on which you can find each topic. The index is found in the back of a book.

Look at this index from the book *Northern Cardinals*. Use it to answer Numbers 14 and 15.

---

### Index

birdfeeder, 37, 71–73

color, 2–8, 12

diet, 32–40

eggs, 5, 44, 61

female, 2, 6–8, 57, 59–61

forests, 21, 24

male, 2, 3–5, 57, 61–63

nests, 22, 41–56

size, 2, 3, 6, 74

song, 2, 9–11, 71

state bird, 2, 21

young, 2, 7, 58, 64–66

---

14. On which pages could you read about cardinals' nests?

    A. 12, 13, and 14

    B. 22 through 24 and 44

    C. 22 and 41 through 56

    D. 37 and 71 through 73

15. On which pages could you read about how big cardinals are?

    A. 2, 3, 4, and 6

    B. 2, 3, 6, and 74

    C. 2, 7, 58, and 64

    D. 71 through 73

**TIP 11: Use the glossary.**

Some books have a **glossary**. This is like a dictionary of every important word in the book. The glossary lists words in alphabetical order. It is found in the back of a book.

Look at this glossary from *All You Ever Wanted to Know about Owls*. Use it to answer Number 16.

**Glossary**

| | |
|---|---|
| **beak** | the bill of a bird |
| **bird of prey** | a bird that kills and eats other animals |
| **burrowing owl** | a small, long-legged owl that nests in holes dug by other animals |
| **habitat** | a place where a plant or animal naturally lives and grows |
| **plumage** | the feathers of a bird |

16. What kind of bird kills and eats other animals?

   A.  bird of prey

   B.  bird of paradise

   C.  burrowing owl

   D.  sparrow

CCSs: W.3.7, W.3.8, W.3.10

 **TIP 12: Use the Internet to find information.**

Most school libraries are connected to the **Internet**, which allows you to "go online" to find a Web site about nearly any kind of information. Your librarian can help you do this. The first step: use a search engine. A **search engine** will search through millions of Web sites to find the ones that have information about your topic.

Search engines will have a place where you can enter key words. **Key words** are words that have the most to do with your topic. If you wanted to find out about the Gulf of Mexico, you would enter the key words "Gulf of Mexico." Once you type the key words and press enter, the search engine will find Web sites about your topic.

Some Web sites have better information than others. Your teacher, parents, or librarian can help you decide which Web sites will give you the best information for your purpose.

17. Which search words would be best to find children's stories?

    A. fairy tales         C. kids' games

    B. U.S. history       D. famous speeches

 **TIP 13: Take notes on your research.**

As you research, write down the important facts, details, and information you find. Write down whatever you think is related to your topic and that you might want to use when you write. You don't need to write in full sentences or every word in the source; you just need to write the information you think you'll use.

When you take notes, be sure to:

- write the source.

- write the author of the source, if this information is given.

- write the page number of the source, if the source has many pages.

You can take notes in your notebook or on note cards. Here is an example.

> *Northern Cardinals, by Red F. Ether*
> *Use sunflower seeds in birdfeeder, p. 72*

**TIP 14:  Organize your notes.**

When you are done taking all your notes from all your sources, you can organize your notes. To organize your notes, think about your purpose.

| If Your Purpose Is . . . | Then You Might Organize Your Notes . . . |
| --- | --- |
| To inform readers about how to build a bird feeder | By each step it takes to build a bird feeder |
| To convince your principal to make lunch breaks longer | By the most convincing information |
| To tell a story | By the beginning, middle, and end of the story |

 **Practice Activity 2**

**Directions:** Look at this student's notes. The student has to write an essay on the ways in which cardinals and blue jays are similar and different. Underline the notes that show how they are similar, and circle the notes that show how they are different. Then, organize the notes by writing them in the lists below.

> www.birds.com
>
> cardinals are red, blue jays are blue
>
> cardinals eat seeds and insects, blue jays eat seeds, insects, and even mice or frogs
>
> <u>Northern Cardinals</u>, by Red F. Ether
> Boy and girl cardinals sing, p. 10
>
> <u>All About Blue Jays</u>, by B. Lou Boyd
> Boy and girl blue jays "sing," p. 29
> Blue jay "song" sounds more like a scream than a song, p. 29

|        **Similar**         |        **Different**        |
| --- | --- |
| _____ | _____ |
| _____ | _____ |
| _____ | _____ |

**Lesson Practice begins on the following page.**

# Ready to Research

On the next page, make a plan for writing step-by-step instructions for making a bird feeder.

## *Writer's Checklist*

✓ **A complete writing plan:**

☐ provides the purpose for your writing.

☐ answers questions about the information you need.

☐ uses people's experience (when possible).

☐ uses many sources, such as encyclopedias, magazines, newspapers, the library, the Internet, and dictionaries.

☐ uses the parts of sources to find the best information (titles, tables of contents, indexes, glossaries).

☐ uses organized notes.

**Directions:** Research how to build a bird feeder. Write your notes below.

_____

_____

_____

_____

_____

_____

_____

_____

_____

_____

_____

_____

_____

_____

**Directions:** Use the graphic organizer below to organize your notes and plan your writing.

| Step 1 |
| --- |
| |
| |
| |

| Step 2 |
| --- |
| |
| |
| |

| Step 3 |
| --- |
| |
| |
| |

| Step 4 |
| --- |
| |
| |
| |

| More Steps . . . |
| --- |
| |
| |
| |

CCSs: W.3.2a, W.3.2b, W.3.2c, W.3.2d, W.3.10

# Lesson 14: Writing Your First Draft

All writers write drafts. A **draft** is a version of something written before it is completed and final. A **first draft** is the first version of any piece of writing. To write your first draft, use your organized notes from when you planned your writing. This lesson includes tips to help you figure out the best way to turn your notes into a first draft.

## TIP 1: Plan your writing.

Not all of your writing will require you to do research. When you plan your writing, you can make an outline, brainstorm, make notes, or complete a graphic organizer, such as a web. These activities are called prewriting. **Prewriting** helps you gather all of the ideas you have about your topic. At this stage, you don't want to worry about what is "right." Instead, you want to let your brain, and your pencil, wander. Write down all of your ideas, and when it is time to draft, organize your ideas. You can refer to your prewriting as you draft to come up with more ideas if you need them.

## TIP 2: Keep the ideas that help you stick to your topic.

How do you sort through a pile of notes? Ask these questions:

- Which ideas are *most* important to support my main idea?
- Which details will *best* support my most important ideas?

Once you have answered these questions, you will be ready to organize a smaller pile of ideas.

## TIP 3: Details and examples say more about the main idea.

The **main idea** is the controlling idea—the idea that controls your story or essay. If your story or essay only had a main idea, it wouldn't be very long or interesting, would it? You need details and examples to describe your topic. With details, you can build on your main idea and show your readers what you want them to see.

For example, maybe you'd like to write a story about a time when your aunt Marian baked a cake. Your main idea, "Aunt Marian baked a cake," wouldn't be much fun to read by itself. But if you added details describing the cake, the kitchen, and even Aunt Marian, it would become a real story!

CCSs: W.3.2a, W.3.2b, W.3.2c, W.3.2d, W.3.10

 **TIP 4: Details give basic facts by using 5W–H information.**

Have you ever heard of the "Five Ws"? They are *who*, *what*, *when*, *where*, and *why*. We often include an H in this kind of information, too: *how*. The 5W-H method is a good place to start when you give your reader details about something. The sentence "Aunt Marian baked a cake" tells you who did something (Aunt Marian) and what she did (baked a cake).

1. Tell something about your school. Include at least three of the 5W-Hs.

_____

_____

_____

_____

_____

**TIP 5: Use linking words to connect your ideas.**

In your first draft, you will be including a lot of ideas and different details. As you write your first draft, you will need to connect one idea to another idea. You'll want your reader to understand your ideas and how they connect!.

To do this, use **linking words**, which show how your different ideas connect.

Here are some linking words you may already know:

| also | another | and |
| but | because | yet |
| more | then | while |

**TIP 6: Some details create a picture in the reader's mind by using the five senses.**

You learned about the five senses in Lesson 7. They are sight, hearing, taste, touch, and smell.

2. To help you remember the five senses, write them on the lines that follow.

_____

_____

_____

_____

When you describe something by giving details that use the five senses, you can create a clear picture in your reader's mind:

Aunt Marian's vanilla cake was three layers tall and had piles of white icing. The strawberries and cream and icing all made a sticky mess in my hair after the food fight, but everything smelled sweet!

3. Describe your school using at least three of the five senses.

_____

_____

_____

Giving a lot of details can make your writing more interesting. Be sure that you use a mixture of the 5W-H, as well as the five senses, to say more about your main idea. This will create the best pictures in your reader's mind.

CCSs: W.3.2a, W.3.2b, W.3.2c, W.3.2d, W.3.10

 **TIP 7: Include a beginning, a middle, and an end.**

You learned in Lesson 6 that stories have a beginning, a middle, and an end. You should include the same elements in your own writing. The **beginning** will most likely include your main idea. The **middle** includes the details and examples that describe the main idea. The **end** ties together your main idea with the details and examples that support it.

You can use an outline to make sure you have a beginning, middle, and end. Take a look at this example:

1. **Beginning**  Stuart is nervous about competing in the school spelling bee.

2. **Middle**  On the way to school, his mother's car gets a flat tire. A woman wearing coveralls arrives in a truck with the word *mechanic* painted on the door and fixes the tire. Finally, Stuart's mother drives him to school just in time for the spelling bee.

3. **End**  Stuart wins the spelling bee by correctly spelling the word *mechanic*.

Of course, you will include more details and examples in the beginning, middle, and end of your story when you write your first draft.

4. Now, think of a story about why a third grader could be late for school. Write an outline that states what will happen in the beginning, middle, and end of that story.

Beginning: _____

_____

Middle: _____

_____

End: _____

_____

**Lesson Practice begins on the following page.**

# Drafting

Use your organized notes from page 153 to draft an essay giving step-by-step instructions for making a bird feeder. Write your draft on the following pages.

## *Writer's Checklist*

✓ **A well-written draft:**

☐ has a beginning with a main idea.

☐ has a middle with details.

☐ gives details about the main idea that stick to the topic.

☐ gives details about the five senses (sight, hearing, taste, touch, and smell).

☐ gives basic facts that answer the questions *who*, *what*, *when*, *where*, *why*, and *how*.

☐ uses linking words to show how ideas connect.

☐ has an ending with a concluding sentence.

**Directions:** Write your first draft on the lines below.

_____

_____

_____

_____

_____

_____

_____

_____

_____

_____

_____

_____

_____

_____

_____

CCSs: W.3.5, W.3.10

# Lesson 15: Revise, Edit, and Publish Your Writing

You learned in Lesson 14 that the **first draft** is the first version of something written. Most writers don't stop after they write down their first draft. They go back to revise and edit their writing to make it the best it can be. When you **revise** your writing, you change it to make it better. You make sure that all of your ideas make sense, that your writing flows, and that it is organized. When you **edit** your writing, you also change it to make it better. You fix any spelling, punctuation, capitalization, and grammar errors.

When you've completed all your revisions and edits, you have a final draft! A **final draft** is a completed draft of your piece. Once you have a final draft, you can publish your piece. When you **publish** your piece, you share it with others. You can print it and hang it up for classmates to see, post it on the Internet, or get it printed in your school newspaper, among other ways.

Have you ever heard people talk like this?

**Kevin:** Allen, have you played the new space-shuttle game?

**Allen:** Did you know the track meet got rained out?

**Kevin:** That storm made the playground look like a huge swimming pool.

**Allen:** So, what did you think of the new space-shuttle game?

Allen and Kevin sure talk about a lot of different things! They begin and end by talking about the new space-shuttle game. But in between, it gets confusing. They bring up a few different ideas.

**How Do You Untwist a Pretzel?**

Sometimes thoughts get twisted around like a pretzel. That's just fine when you're thinking to yourself. Sometimes it even works when you're talking with a good friend. It doesn't work very well in writing, though. When you write, you need to untwist your ideas. Stick to the main topic so your readers aren't confused.

This is where revising comes in. You revise after you have written your ideas down for the first time. You read back over what you've written and make sure it says exactly what you want it to say.

Read the following tips to help you revise your work.

 ## TIP 1:  Remember your audience and purpose.

Ask yourself, *Who am I writing for?* and *Why am I writing?* You may be writing a story to entertain your classmates, a letter to update your grandparents about your soccer team, or an essay to describe a book for your teacher.

As you revise your writing, make sure that you keep your audience in mind and that you remember why you are writing. Keeping your purpose and audience in mind will make writing more fun and more focused.

 ## TIP 2:  Make sure that each sentence tells something about your topic.

Look back at what Allen and Kevin say to each other. Their main topic was the new space-shuttle game. But they also talked about the track meet, the rainstorm, and the flooded playground. If Allen and Kevin were characters in a story, readers would probably have a hard time following along.

Now it's your turn to practice sticking to the topic.

Read the following paragraph. Its topic, or main idea, is food for butterflies.

---

(1) A butterfly stopping for lunch will probably dine on a flower. (2) Many butterflies have a long, straw-like tube they use to suck up sweet juices from flowers. (3) Humans use straws to suck up sweet things, too, such as sodas and shakes. (4) Some kinds of butterflies don't have juice for lunch, though. (5) Some butterflies eat what's left of dead animals. (6) When a butterfly stands on something, it usually holds its wings together. (7) A moth, on the other hand, stands with its wings spread open. (8) Other kinds of butterflies don't eat anything at all! (9) They use energy that when they were caterpillars they stored. (10) Caterpillars are very cute.

---

1.  Now go back and cross out the sentences that don't tell about the main topic. Remember, the topic is food for butterflies. Write the numbers for each sentence you crossed out on the line below.

_____

CCSs: W.3.5, W.3.6, W.3.10

Now reread the paragraph to yourself. This time, skip the sentences you crossed out. Doesn't it make more sense now?

Do the same thing to your writing. Read it carefully to see if all your details and examples relate to the main idea. Then take out any information that does not support your topic.

 **TIP 3: Add more to your writing if you need to.**

When you read over your writing, you may find that you forgot to put in some important facts or details. Maybe you need to add a word, a few words, a sentence, or even a whole paragraph.

2.  Let's say you wrote the paragraph on page 162 about food for butterflies. You discover that you left out some facts. You forgot to say that some butterflies eat something called *pollen* from flowers. Add a sentence about this fact to the paragraph. Write your sentence on the lines that follow.

    _____

    _____

    Between which two sentences would you add this new fact?

    _____

**TIP 4:  Reword some sentences to make them clearer.**

When you **reword** something, you find another way to say it. Sometimes, when you write something for the first time, you can confuse your readers. When you revise, you can reword confusing writing and make it easier to understand. You can change a word, a group of words, a sentence, or larger parts of your writing.

Sometimes you may simply want to use a better, or more specific, word than the one you are already using. You can use a dictionary to help you find the perfect word for what you want to say.

3.  Reread this sentence from the "food for butterflies" paragraph.

    (9) They use energy that when they were caterpillars they stored.

    Now reword the sentence to make it easier to understand.

    _____

    _____

 **Practice Activity 1**

**Directions:** Imagine that your school is going to buy new things for the playground. The principal wants to find out what each student would like the school to buy. A few ideas include: a wooden castle, a rope, a tall slide, a ladder, or tire swing.

Pick what you think the school should buy. It might be the swings, a slide, or something else you like to play on. Tell about this thing on the lines below.

_____

_____

_____

Next, write two or three reasons the school should buy this equipment.

_____

_____

CCSs: W.3.5, W.3.6, W.3.10

## ✎ Practice Activity 2

**Directions:** Now use your ideas to write a letter to your principal. Try to get your principal to choose your idea. Remember to give two or three reasons that support your choice, or main idea. Write your letter on the lines below. Remember that your audience is your principal. Your purpose for writing is to explain why the principal should buy the playground item you want.

_____

_____

_____

_____

_____

_____

_____

_____

_____

_____

_____

_____

_____

_____

_____

Review the following tips to edit and publish your work.

## TIP 5: Edit your work.

You've already done the hardest parts of writing: planning, drafting, and revising. Now it's time to edit. **Editing** means looking for mistakes in punctuation, capitalization, grammar, and spelling. Carefully, reread your writing. Try to look for one type of mistake at a time. For example, you might look at spelling, then punctuation, and so on. You will learn more about these skills in Unit 3.

## TIP 6: Use a checklist to make sure your writing is as good as it can be.

After you've made all of the changes that stand out, you can use a checklist to make your writing even better. A checklist is a list of things to check before you finish a writing assignment.

---

✓ **Revising Checklist:**

☐  I have thought about my purpose for writing.

☐  I have thought about who I am writing for.

☐  I have a main idea that controls my writing.

☐  All of the details and examples support the main idea.

☐  I have added details and examples where they are needed.

☐  My writing is clear and easy to understand.

☐  There is a clear beginning, middle, and end to my writing.

☐  All the words are spelled correctly.

☐  All the punctuation is correctly used.

☐  If I used a computer, I correctly typed everything.

---

## TIP 7: Publish your writing for others to see.

When you've completed all your revisions and edits, you have a final draft! Now you can publish your writing to share it with others. Writers can publish their work by typing their work using a computer. But they can also publish their work in many other ways.

4. Think of the different ways writers publish their work. Write down two ways writers publish their work using technology.

_____

_____

Write down two ways writers publish their work *without* using technology.

_____

_____

5. In what way would you *least* want to publish your own writing? Why?

_____

_____

_____

In what way would you *most* want to publish your own writing? Why?

_____

_____

_____

6. Pick one of the ways you listed in Number 4. Then, describe what supplies you would need to publish this way. Also, describe what kind of help you might need from an adult to publish this way.

_____

_____

_____

## Lesson Practice begins on the following page.

# Revising and Editing

Read through the essay draft you wrote on pages 159 and 160. Revise and edit your draft. Write your final copy on the following pages.

## Writer's Checklist

✔ **A well-written essay:**

☐ has a clear purpose.

☐ keeps the audience in mind.

☐ shows organization.

☐ includes developed ideas with enough supporting details.

☐ includes linking words between ideas.

☐ includes correct grammar and sentence structure.

**Directions:** Write your final copy on the lines below.

_____

_____

_____

_____

_____

_____

_____

_____

_____

_____

_____

_____

_____

_____

CCSs: W.3.3a, W.3.3d, W.3.4, W.3.10

# Lesson 16: Writing Narratives

A **narrative** is a story. It can be a made-up story or a true story. All narratives must have three important things: characters, a setting, and a plot.

- **Characters** are the people, animals, or creatures in a story.
- The **setting** is the place and time in which the story happens.
- The **plot** is what happens to the characters in the story.

If you put all three of these things together, you have a story. In a story, something happens (the plot) to someone (a character), somewhere and at some time (the setting).

Let's review the parts of a story more closely. Read the following tips.

## TIP 1: A story can have a narrator and must have characters.

The person telling the story is the **narrator**. You may think that the narrator is the writer, but writers get to write from all different points of view. You've probably read books where an animal tells a story—but the writer isn't an animal! Writers can have their narrators be all sorts of things: other people, kids, adults, boys, girls, animals, plants, places.

Who is acting in the story? These are the **characters**. True stories and made-up stories must have characters. You and your family could be the characters in your story. Whoever your characters are, be sure to give details so your reader will know what they are like.

## Practice Activity 1

**Directions:** For each sentence below, identify the narrator and the characters.

1. Each morning, I woke up and hopped to the lettuce patch. My brother, Big Ears, would come with me, and we would eat our fill of fresh lettuce greens for breakfast!

Narrator: _____

Character: _____

2. The election of President Lincoln was one of many things that led to the American Civil War. Many states disagreed with Lincoln's plans and policies.

Narrator: _____

Character: _____

3. I have spent years working in the movies. I can tell you all sorts of tales. How actors demand special water and food! How directors and producers argue! I have some secrets to tell.

Narrator: _____

Character: _____

**TIP 2: Show what your characters think, feel, say, and do.**

To write an interesting story, you should show lots of details about your characters. You can describe what your characters think, feel, and do. You can also use dialogue to show what your characters say.

Here are two examples of the same story. Which one is more fun to read?

### Story 1

Sam and Mia walked into the cave. The cave was dark. There were puddles of water. The walls of the cave were painted with pictures.

### Story 2

Sam and Mia were a little nervous as they walked into the dark, shadowy cave. "Watch out for the puddles, Sam," said Mia. Ben walked around the puddle. *That would have been awful,* thought Sam to himself, *to have wet shoes in this dark cave.* Sam and Mia saw amazing pictures painted on the cave walls. They were orange and white. "Whoa!" said Sam and Mia together, as they looked at a huge cave painting of a beautiful orange sun.

1. Which story is more fun to read? Why?

_____

_____

CCSs: W.3.3a, W.3.3b, W.3.3c, W.3.3d, W.3.4, W.3.10

 **TIP 3:** **Use words and phrases to tell the sequence of events.**

As you write a story, you will tell readers about different events. You want readers to know the order in which the events take place. You can use sequence words to make sure readers know the sequence of the events in your story.

Here are some sequence words that you may already know:

| | | |
|---|---|---|
| first | second | third |
| last | finally | then |
| before | later | after |

 ## Practice Activity 2

**Directions:** Read the sentences. For each example, write a sequence word that best shows the order of events on the line. Use the sequence words shown on this page.

1. Rascal, our new dog, got out of his leash. _____ he went running down the hill to swim in the pond.

2. _____ Ted went outside, he checked the weather and grabbed an umbrella.

 **TIP 4:** **Use words that clearly and completely describe your topic.**

Word choice is important in every kind of writing, but is *very* important when writing stories about things that have really happened. These kinds of writings call for exactly the right words.

For example, instead of saying "an airplane," you might be more exact and say "a double-decker, 853-seat, four-engine Airbus A380."

173

**TIP 5: Add descriptions.**

Sometimes you will need to write a description or will want to describe a setting or character in your story. No matter what kind of writing you're doing, don't forget to use your five senses. Tell how things looked, sounded, felt, and so on. You don't need to tell about every little thing. A few key details will help the reader "see" (or even "taste," "hear," "touch," or "smell") the story.

Here are two examples of the same story. Which one is more fun to read?

### Story 1

Last year, my mom made me take piano lessons. I didn't want to take them because my older sister took piano lessons and didn't like them. After my first lesson, I ended up liking to play the piano.

### Story 2

I was watching TV one Saturday afternoon when my mom said, "Denise, I've signed you up to start piano lessons with Mrs. Leonard." I told my mom I didn't like this idea. My big sister, Lisa, had taken piano lessons for two years with Mrs. Leonard. Lisa always complained about how Mrs. Leonard made her play boring music over and over again.

"Well, just give it a try," Mom said.

The day of the first lesson came. I figured I'd go to a couple of lessons, and then I could quit. I knocked on Mrs. Leonard's door, and she let me in. She was as old as my grandma, but she didn't look like any grandma I'd ever seen. She had bright red hair and wore a long, shiny dress with blue butterflies on it.

She led me to the old piano that sat in the corner of her living room. She took my hand and arranged three of my fingers on three of the piano keys.

"Now, push the keys down at the same time," she said.

When I did, a wonderful sound came out of the old piano. I couldn't believe I had made that sound by myself.

"How does that feel?" Mrs. Leonard asked.

"Great!" I said. From the time I heard that first sound, I knew I'd want to play piano until I was as old as Mrs. Leonard.

2. Which story is more fun to read? Why?

_____

_____

CCSs: W.3.3a, W.3.3b, W.3.3c, W.3.3d, W.3.4, W.3.10

 **Practice Activity 3**

**Directions:** Your teacher has asked you to write a made-up story about two kids who spend a day at the beach. Each of the following leaves stands for a detail from your story. Draw a line to connect the details to the part of the caterpillar where each idea belongs.

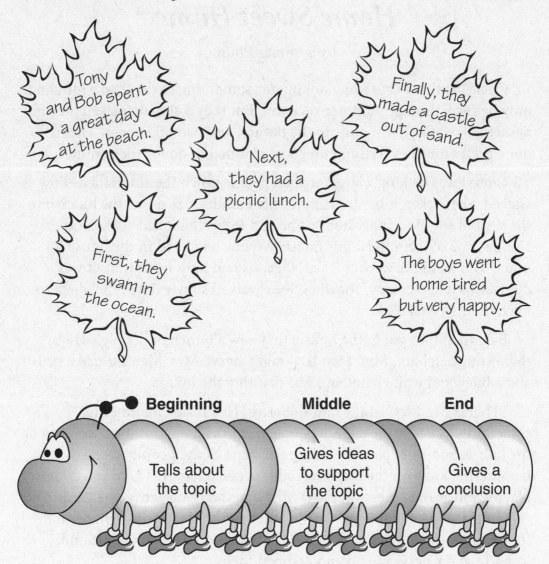

**Lesson Practice begins on the following page.**

175

# Writing Narrative Essays

**Directions:** Read the following narrative story. This story shows what you learned in this lesson.

## *Home Sweet Home*

### by Summer Phun

Cheryl and Roberto were looking for something to do. It was July, and only halfway through summer vacation. But they'd already played lots of basketball, watched TV, gone to the library, and had bike races. They'd done pretty much everything they had planned to do for the summer.

Cheryl was kicking a large, striped pebble down the sidewalk as they walked. She kicked it hard. Then, it rolled all the way down the block into the yard of the old, empty house. She and Roberto looked at each other. Neither one of them liked this house. No one had lived in the house for years. The windows were cracked. Pigeons had built nests in it. It was dirty, stinky, and creepy. Together, they walked slowly down the block to fetch their striped rock.

But when they got to the house, they saw a bunch of people! "Hey, there's our neighbor, Mrs. Mendez," said Cheryl. Mrs. Mendez had a brush and a bucket of white paint and was painting the house.

"There's Mr. McCarthy," said Roberto. "He's inside hammering something." There were a lot of people from the neighborhood working on the house. Some people were fixing the steps. Some people were hammering away on the roof. Everyone seemed happy. There was a radio playing music. Just then, they saw Mrs. Lena walking across the yard carrying a large container of small plants. But there were too many, and they were about to fall out of her arms. Before they fell to the ground, Roberto and Cheryl ran up and grabbed them.

"Thank you, kids!" she said. "Could you help me carry these over near the steps? We're going to plant them around the front of the house to make it look pretty."

"Sure thing," Roberto said. "But could you tell us what all this is?" Roberto looked around at everyone busily working.

"This is the Home-Sweet-Home group," Mrs. Lena explained. "We're neighbors who come together to fix these rotten houses into nice houses. Then, people who can't afford brand-new houses can live here. The neighborhood gets to have a nice house and a nice new neighbor, and the person gets to have a nice home."

Cheryl and Roberto looked at each other.

"I think we found something fun and interesting to do for the rest of the summer," Cheryl whispered to Roberto. Roberto nodded and grinned. They couldn't wait to get started painting, planting flowers, and helping make a happy new home for someone in need.

# Narrative Writing Prompt

Write a narrative story about a time when you did something new or tried something different. Plan your story on the following page. Write your final story on pages 179 and 180.

## *Writer's Checklist*

✔ **A well-written narrative:**

☐ has a narrator and characters.

☐ shows what the characters think, feel, and do.

☐ uses dialogue to show what the characters say.

☐ clearly describes a setting.

☐ has a clear plot.

☐ has a beginning, a middle, and an end.

☐ uses sequence words to clearly show the order of events.

☐ includes specific details and descriptions.

**Directions:** Plan your story in the space below.

| Beginning |
|---|
| |
| |
| |
| |
| |

| Middle |
|---|
| |
| |
| |
| |
| |

| End |
|---|
| |
| |
| |
| |
| |

**Directions:** Write your story on the lines below.

_____

_____

_____

_____

_____

_____

_____

_____

_____

_____

_____

_____

_____

_____

_____

CCSs: W.3.2a, W.3.2b, W.3.4, W.3.10

# Lesson 17: Writing to Inform

When you write to inform, you write to share information with your readers. You can decide what type of information you want to share, but be sure to write clearly.

When you write an informational essay, you can write for a lot of different purposes. For example, you can explain step-by-step how to build a go-cart or describe the results of a science experiment. Your readers will read what you write in order to learn what information you have to share.

Writing to inform is easy, and it can be lots of fun. Just follow these tips:

 **TIP 1:  First, choose a topic.**

Your teacher may assign a topic to you. Or, you may choose a topic that is interesting to you. Pick something that makes you curious or something that you will enjoy learning more about.

 **TIP 2:  Next, gather your information.**

Encyclopedias, newspapers, magazines, books, and the Internet are all great sources of information. You also may want to interview someone who knows a lot about your topic.

Ask your teacher or librarian for more ideas about gathering information.

1.  Imagine that you need to write a paper about popular hobbies among students at your elementary school. Which of these people would not be a good source?

    A.  a teacher at your school

    B.  a librarian at your library

    C.  the head of a hobby club at school

    D.  your older sister in high school

 **TIP 3:  Organize your information.**

Sort the information you have gathered.

- What is the main idea?

- What are the important ideas that support the main idea?

- What are the details that support each important idea?

**181**

Connect the supporting ideas and details in an organized way. Put the most important information first.

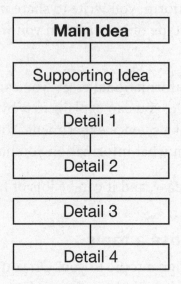

```
┌─────────────────────┐
│     Main Idea       │
└─────────────────────┘
          │
┌─────────────────────┐
│   Supporting Idea   │
└─────────────────────┘
          │
┌─────────────────────┐
│      Detail 1       │
└─────────────────────┘
          │
┌─────────────────────┐
│      Detail 2       │
└─────────────────────┘
          │
┌─────────────────────┐
│      Detail 3       │
└─────────────────────┘
          │
┌─────────────────────┐
│      Detail 4       │
└─────────────────────┘
```

 **TIP 4:  Decide which information stays and which goes.**

We can often gather a lot of information about a topic; but not all of it relates back to the main idea. It's important to get rid of this information so the reader will not be confused.

2.  If you were writing a report about a concert you attended, which of the following details should be left out?

    A.  what type of music was played

    B.  how many people were there

    C   that you had a hot dog with relish

    D.  how long the concert lasted

 **TIP 5:  Put your information into paragraphs.**

Organize your paragraphs in the same order that you organized your information. It is very important to use your own words. Don't copy someone else's words.

**Example:** Anthony wants to earn a merit badge from the Boys & Girls Club. One way he can earn a badge is to give the club useful information about animals. He has decided to explain to the club how to choose a pet.

CCSs: W.3.2a, W.3.2b, W.3.4, W.3.10

Anthony has gathered information from many sources. He has read about pets in an encyclopedia and in other books from the library. He has visited a pet store and talked to the people there. He has even talked to a veterinarian, a special kind of doctor just for pets. Here is how Anthony has decided to organize the information he has found.

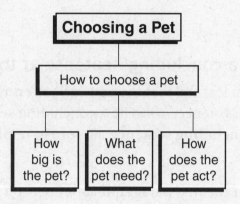

Here is a draft of some of the information Anthony wants to give to his club members.

There are many important things to think about when choosing a pet. How big is the pet? If it is very big, it will probably need a big place to live. A horse will not be very happy in a small apartment! What does the pet need? Also, ask yourself: How much work is it to take care of the pet? If no one is at your house all day, you might pick a goldfish. They don't get very lonely. How does the pet act? Is it friendly to people? Will it need a lot of training? Will it gobble up your little sister? Be sure to choose a pet that fits in with you and your family.

When choosing a pet, think about how much work it will take to care for the pet.

There are many different kinds of pets to choose from. There are also many things to think about when choosing a pet. Be careful to make a choice that is right for you and your future pet.

**TIP 6:  Use pictures to show your ideas.**

You might find it helpful to draw a picture to show your ideas to your readers.

You could show your ideas in a lot of different ways. You might draw a picture, diagram, graph, table, or chart. You can also paste pictures or images cut from magazines.

**TIP 7:  Write a concluding sentence at the end of your essay.**

In Lesson 14, you learned that the end of your essay ties together your main idea and details. Also, you need to write a concluding sentence at the end of your essay. In your **concluding sentence**, be sure to remind your reader of your main idea.

3.  Look back at the first paragraph about pets on page 183. Underline the concluding sentence in this paragraph.

**Lesson Practice begins on the following page.**

# Writing Informational Essays

**Directions:** Read the following informational essay. This essay shows what you learned in this lesson.

## *A School for Hot Dogs*

### by Rella Yish

Summertime. Grills. Baseball games. Birthday parties. Hot dogs are a popular food to eat for many reasons. You can make them at home or buy them from a hot dog cart. But, did you know that you can go to school to learn how to run your own hot dog cart? It's true. The school is called Hot Dog University. At this special school, people can learn all they need to know to run their own successful hot dog cart business.

At Hot Dog University, students come together in small classes. They learn how to cook hot dogs using the little kitchen in a hot dog cart. They also learn how to run their own business. For example, they learn about how much running a hot dog cart costs and how to get permits to have a food cart.

All the courses at Hot Dog University are taught by one man—Mark Reitman. Mark Reitman is known as the Professor of Hot Dogs. How did Reitman learn so much about hot dogs and hot dog carts? He spent many years of his life cooking up and serving food to hungry people at a restaurant. Also, for many years, he had his own hot dog cart business. After working so hard for so many years, he decided to help other people figure out the tools of the trade. That is why he started Hot Dog University in 2006. Since that time, he's trained many people in how to run a hot dog cart business.

You might think that running a hot dog cart is easy. But it's not. People who run a hot dog cart have to figure out a lot of things. They need freezers to keep the uncooked hot dogs cold. They need tanks of fuel to cook the hot dogs and keep them hot. Sometimes pipes leak water. Sometimes the wheels on a cart don't work well. After all that, they need to have all the toppings people want on their hot dogs: ketchup, mustard, sauerkraut, and pickle relish.

Running your own hot dog cart business can be both difficult and rewarding. Mark Reitman tries to help people learn the skills to handle all the ups and downs. Going to Hot Dog University is the first step in being a successful hot dog cart business owner.

# Informational Writing Prompt

Write an informational essay that gives clear information about a type of food or a class at school. Plan your essay on the following page. Write your final essay on pages 188 and 189.

## *Writer's Checklist*

✓ **A well-written essay:**

☐ contains a clear topic.

☐ contains a lot of information and details.

☐ is organized in paragraphs.

☐ contains only information about the topic.

☐ uses pictures to show your ideas when necessary.

☐ has a concluding sentence.

**Directions:** Plan your informational essay in the spaces below.

| **Main Idea:** |
| --- |
| _____ |
| _____ |

| Supporting Idea: |
| --- |
| _____ |
| _____ |

| Detail 1: |
| --- |
| _____ |
| _____ |
| _____ |

| Detail 2: |
| --- |
| _____ |
| _____ |
| _____ |

| Detail 3: |
| --- |
| _____ |
| _____ |
| _____ |

| Detail 4: |
| --- |
| _____ |
| _____ |
| _____ |

**Directions:** Write your essay on the lines below.

_____

_____

_____

_____

_____

_____

_____

_____

_____

_____

_____

_____

_____

_____

_____

_____

_____

_____

_____

_____

_____

_____

_____

_____

_____

_____

_____

_____

_____

_____

CCSs: W.3.1a, W.3.1b, W.3.1c, W.3.1d, W.3.4, W.3.10

# Lesson 18: Writing Opinions

When you write an opinion essay, you write to share an opinion. An **opinion** is a feeling. Different people can have different feelings about the same thing. For example, "The moon is very beautiful" is an opinion.

There are many examples of opinion essays, such as advertisements and certain articles in newspapers called editorials.

When you write an opinion essay, you write to clearly state your opinion and also provide a lot of reasons, details, and facts that support your opinion. A **fact** is an idea that everyone can agree on, such as "The moon is 225,744 miles from Earth."

 **TIP 1:  A fact can be checked to see if it is correct. An opinion cannot be checked.**

When writers use facts, they're saying, "This is true. Go ahead and check it out if you don't think it's correct."

If your friend Mickey says, "My bicycle is blue," he's using a fact. You can check the color of Mickey's bicycle. Remember, a fact does not have to be true, but it has to make a statement that can be checked. For example, "Louisville has a population of 36 people" is certainly not true, but it is a fact because it can be checked. Facts use words that mean the same thing to everybody, such as *brown*, *round*, *square*, *north*, *up*, and *down*.

An **opinion** cannot be checked. Mickey might say, "My bicycle is fast." How fast? Faster than his sister's bicycle? Faster than a race car? Faster than an airplane? To *him* it might be fast, but to *you* it might seem slow. Words such as *beautiful*, *wonderful*, *fast*, and *slow* are opinion words. Opinion words cannot be checked, because they mean different things to different people.

CCSs: W.3.1a, W.3.1b, W.3.4, W.3.10

The following chart shows you some opinion words to watch out for.

| Examples of Opinion Words | | |
|---|---|---|
| beautiful | scary | exciting |
| ugly | funny | yucky |
| best | wonderful | boring |
| silly | awful | expensive |

1. Read the following sentence.

   Rollo is a very smart dog.

   Now write a sentence about how a smart dog acts.

   _____

   _____

   _____

   _____

   _____

   _____

2. When your teacher tells you to do so, look at a classmate's answer. Does "a very smart dog" mean the same thing to every student?

   _____

   _____

**TIP 2: Convince your readers that you are correct.**

Imagine that you have just hurried through another lunch period. The lines in the lunchroom moved too slowly. It took so long to get your food that you had only two minutes left to eat it. You decide to write a letter to your principal asking her if she could make the lunch period 10 minutes longer.

You must do more than ask the principal to make the lunch period longer. You also need to explain why your idea is a good one. Give her some reasons why the lunch period needs to be longer.

Your letter to the principal might read like this:

---

January 18, 2010

Dear Principal Hansen,

I think the lunch period should be ten minutes longer. The lines in the lunchroom move too slowly. Some people don't have time to eat their lunch. When people don't eat, they get hungry. When people are hungry, they have trouble learning in class. A longer lunch period could help students get better grades.

Thank you,

Lynne Ann Greene

---

When you write to win others over to your way of thinking, you must give your readers reasons to make them agree with what you say. Your opinion essay can take the form of a letter, an essay, or a speech.

**TIP 3: Share your opinion in the beginning of your essay.**

Remember from Lesson 4 that the **main idea** is the controlling idea. When writing an opinion essay, your opinion is your controlling idea, so your opinion is your main idea.

Be sure to write your opinion (or main idea) in the beginning of your opinion essay. This lets your readers know early on what your opinion is. Then all the details and information you put in the middle of your essay will make sense to your readers.

 **TIP 4: Organize your information.**

So most likely you have a lot of reasons, information, and facts that support your opinion. Now, you need to organize your information.

Ask yourself these questions:

- What is my strongest reason?
- Would my readers be most convinced if they read all my reasons?
- Would my readers be most convinced if they read only certain reasons?
- What reason might my reader have to not agree with my opinion?

Then, organize your information in the following way:

**Beginning:** My Main Idea (Opinion)

**Middle:**

- First set of reasons or information that support my opinion
- Second set of reasons or information that support my opinion
- Set of reasons why my reader might disagree, and why readers should agree with my opinion instead

**End:** My concluding sentence

Here is an example of a student's opinion essay that was printed in the school newspaper. It has the opposite opinion of Lynne Ann Greene's letter to the principal.

While Lynne Ann Greene thinks that Principal Hansen should make lunch longer, I disagree. If the lunch period is longer, that means that kids will have less time in important classes. So, we'll have less time learning important stuff like math or science. Or, we'll have less time outside or in gym class. Therefore, making lunchtime longer would not be good! While Lynne is right that students need to eat to do well, I don't think making the lunch period longer is the right way to go. The line does move slowly. I think our school should add an extra line. That would help everyone pay for their food more quickly and have more time to eat without losing time for classes. That's why I disagree with Lynne's idea.

 **TIP 5: Add reasons, details, and facts that develop your opinion.**

When you read over your first draft, be sure to include important facts or details. You can add a word, a few words, a sentence, or even a whole paragraph.

3. Let's say you wrote the paragraph about adding the lunch line. You find out that you left out some facts. You forgot to say that some kids bring their lunch and do not even stand in the lunch line. Write your sentence on the lines that follow.

_____

_____

Where would you add this new fact?

_____

_____

CCSs: W.3.1c, W.3.1d, W.3.4, W.3.10

 **TIP 6:  Use linking words to connect your reasons.**

In your first draft, you will need to connect your reasons. To do this, use linking words. **Linking words** show how your different reasons connect to support your opinion.

Here are some linking words you might already know:

| | | |
|---|---|---|
| because | therefore | in order to |
| since | for example | but |

 **TIP 7:  Write a concluding sentence at the end of your essay.**

When writing an opinion essay, you should say your opinion again in your concluding sentence. But when you do, say it in a slightly new or different way. By beginning and ending your essay with your opinion, your reader will really understand what you are saying.

4.  Look back at the paragraph on page 194 about adding another lunch line. Underline the concluding sentence.

**Lesson Practice begins on the following page.**

# Writing Opinion Essays

**Directions:** Read the following article about having a farm at school. Then respond to the writing prompt.

# *Our School Should Be a Farm*

by Tom A. Toe

Right now, every day across America, kids eat breakfast and lunch at school. In a week, a lot of kids will eat 10 out of 21 meals at their schools. That's almost half! Yet, some of the food at school isn't so healthy or fresh. That's why I think our school should start its own farm in the extra back lot!

First of all, the food would be healthy. Right now, we don't get to eat a lot of fresh vegetables with our lunches. Sometimes, there's canned corn or canned beans. It's hard for the school to get fresh vegetables. But vegetables grown just a couple feet away from the cafeteria would be super fresh. It would be better for students to eat more vegetables. Growing kids need healthy food. Kids eating almost half their food at the school definitely need the food to be healthy.

Second of all, the food would be free. There's always stuff in the news about how schools don't have enough money. If we had a farm, the school wouldn't have to spend so much money on buying food. The money that would be spent on buying food could be spent on other things. We could have more books in our library. Or, we could have more art supplies and sports supplies to use.

Now some people might say that school is a place for learning. They think that having a farm at school doesn't make sense. But a farm is a great place to learn. The students could take care of the farm. The science teachers can use the farm for science class. The farm could be a place for students to learn about plants and insects.

So as you can see, having a farm at school is a great idea. A farm would be a place for learning. And the farm would give us healthy and free food. So, that's why I think we should start farming at our school!

# Opinion Essay Prompt

Write a persuasive essay that explains an argument for or against having a garden at school. Plan your essay on the following page. Write your final essay on pages 199 and 200.

## Writer's Checklist

✔ **A well-written opinion essay:**

☐ introduces a clear opinion.

☐ supports the opinion with clear reasons and facts.

☐ tries to convince readers.

☐ is organized.

☐ uses linking words to connect reasons.

☐ ends with a concluding sentence.

**Directions:** Plan your essay in the spaces below.

1. **Beginning: My Main Idea (Opinion)**

   _____

2. **Middle:**

   a.  First set of reasons or information that support my opinion

   _____

   _____

   _____

   b.  Second set of reasons or information that support my opinion

   _____

   _____

   _____

   c.  Set of reasons why my reader might disagree, and why readers should agree with my opinion instead

   _____

   _____

   _____

3. **End: My concluding sentence**

   _____

   _____

**Directions:** Write your essay on the lines below.

_____

_____

_____

_____

_____

_____

_____

_____

_____

_____

_____

_____

_____

_____

_____

_____

# UNIT 3

# Language

When you write, you can be sure your readers will understand what you are saying by using language correctly.

By using language correctly, you use:

- sentences to express your ideas.
- punctuation to express your feelings.
- words to express the meaning you want.

In this unit, you'll learn how to use language correctly so that you can be sure your feelings, opinions, and ideas are clear to readers. You will learn how to build strong sentences, capitalize and punctuate correctly, and spell correctly.

## In This Unit

Building Strong Sentences

Capitalization and Punctuation

Spelling Tools

**201**

CCSs: L.3.1a, L.3.1f

# Lesson 19: Building Strong Sentences

Words are a lot like connecting building blocks. If you don't put the blocks together correctly, they'll fall apart. You won't have a strong building or structure. It's the same with words. If you don't put words together correctly, your sentences will also fall apart. But if you are careful in putting your words together, you will build strong sentences.

A strong sentence tells readers what happened and who or what was involved in the action. That means that a strong sentence has both a subject and a verb. The **subject** is who or what does the action, and the **verb** is the action. In this lesson, you'll learn how to put these kinds of words together so that your sentences stick together like a strong castle made of building blocks.

 **TIP 1: A complete sentence must have a subject and a verb.**

As you know, the **subject** is who or what does the action in a sentence, and the **verb** is the action. There is always a noun or pronoun in the subject.

Read the following sentences, which show how these different kinds of words connect.

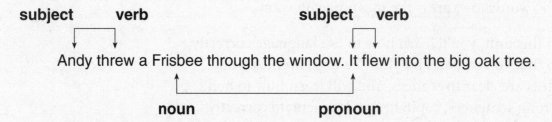

- A **noun** (*Andy*) is a person, place, or thing.

- A **pronoun** (*It*) is a word that takes the place of a noun (*Frisbee*). The word *It* is the subject of the second sentence.

- The **verb** (*threw, flew*) is the part of the sentence that tells what the subject does.

CCSs: L.3.1a, L.3.1f

 **TIP 2: Make subjects and verbs match.**

Subject / verb agreement is when subjects agree in number with verbs. Verbs must match their subjects. A **singular** subject means there is only one thing, such as *puppy*, *girl*, or *plant*. It takes a singular verb, such as *grows*. Most singular verbs end in *s*.

A **plural** subject is more than one thing, such as *puppies*, *girls*, or *plants*. A plural subject takes a plural verb, such as *grow*.

Look at the following examples.

| Singular | Plural |
|---|---|
| The <u>onion</u> *makes* my eyes water. | The <u>onions</u> *make* my eyes water. |
| The <u>bug</u> *jumps.* | The <u>bugs</u> *jump.* |
| The <u>tulip</u> *is* my favorite flower. | <u>Tulips</u> *are* my favorite flowers. |

 **Practice Activity 1**

**Directions:** In the following sentences, circle the verb that matches the subject.

**Example:** The bird in that maple tree ( (is) / are ) a blue jay.

1. *Mother Goose and Grimm* comic strips ( make / makes ) me fall over laughing.

2. All of my cousins, except Cecil, ( has / have ) dark, black hair.

3. Pineapples and kiwi fruit ( is / are ) both delicious with chocolate ice cream.

4. The bumpers on that car ( is / are ) muddy.

**TIP 3:  Know your verb tenses.**

A verb tells readers not only what action happened but when the action happened. A verb's **tense** lets the reader know what happened in the past, what is happening now, or what will happen in the future. It is important to make sure that the verbs you use are all in the right tense.

Verbs in the **past tense** tell about actions that have already happened.

> Yesterday, we <u>painted</u>. Or: Yesterday, we <u>were painting</u>.

Verbs in the **present tense** describe actions that are happening now.

> We <u>paint</u>. Or: We are <u>painting</u>.

Verbs in the **future tense** describe actions that will happen in the future.

> Tomorrow, we <u>will paint</u>. Or: Tomorrow, we <u>are going to paint</u>.

 **Practice Activity 2**

**Directions:** In the following sentences, circle the correct verb.

**Example:** Heidi used to like tennis best, but now she ( (likes) / liked / will like ) soccer more than tennis.

1. E. J. ( hides / hid / will hide ) from his sister last week.

2. We ( kick / kicked / will kick ) the soccer ball tomorrow.

3. My sister ( is / was / will be ) four years old next week.

4. He always ( washes / washed / will wash ) his hands before he eats.

5. How do you ( like / liked / will like ) your new teacher?

**TIP 4: Some past-tense verbs look strange.**

Most verbs end in *-ed* when used in the past tense. For example, the past tense of *jump* is *jumped*. But some verbs are a little strange. They do not end in *-ed* when used in the past tense. These kinds of verbs are called **irregular verbs**.

The following table lists many irregular verbs that we use every day.

**Irregular Verbs**

| Verbs | Past Tense | Verbs | Past Tense |
|-------|------------|-------|------------|
| be | **was, were** | know | **knew** |
| begin | **began** | leave | **left** |
| bring | **brought** | make | **made** |
| come | **came** | say | **said** |
| drink | **drank** | send | **sent** |
| go | **went** | stand | **stood** |
| have | **had** | tell | **told** |

 **Practice Activity 3**

**Directions:** Circle the correct past-tense form of the following irregular verbs.

1. My mom ( telled / told ) me it was time for bed.

2. Shana ( drinked / drank ) a chocolate milk shake last night.

3. Marty ( went / goed ) to Lucy's birthday party.

4. I never ( knew / knowed ) the Aquarius Mountains were in Arizona.

5. Leah ( broke / breaked ) the school record for sit-ups.

**TIP 5: Use adverbs to describe actions.**

**Adverbs** are words that show when, where, and how things happen. Adverbs describe the verbs. Here are some examples of adverbs:

**when:** Kyle made up a song <u>today</u>.

**where:** Cheryl climbed <u>over</u> the fence.

**how:** He chewed <u>slowly</u>.

**how (much):** The water is <u>very</u> clear.

**how (often):** She screams <u>every day</u> to get her way.

Adverbs also show how things are alike or different.

**alike:** Our dog snores <u>as</u> loudly as a jet engine.

**different:** Dougie reads <u>better</u> than he does math.

**different:** Having fun is <u>more</u> important than winning.

**different:** No one dresses <u>more</u> beautifully than Olivia.

 **Practice Activity 4**

**Directions:** Fill in the blanks with adverbs.

1. I opened the envelope _____.

2. The wizard waved his wand _____.

3. Diana ate her lunch _____.

4. There has _____ been a superhero better than Superman.

5. Gary's cat, Steve, is _____ smart as a person.

Here are some more examples of adverbs that can be used to compare things. Pay attention to their spelling changes.

Some adverbs are changed into comparing words by adding *-er* or *-est* to the base word.

| hard | harder | hardest |
| soon | sooner | soonest |

A few adverbs do not keep their root words when changed into comparing words.

| well | better | best |
| bad | worse | worst |

Most adverbs need an extra word (usually another adverb) to turn them into comparing words.

| happily | more happily | most happily |
| safely | less safely | least safely |

## ✎ Practice Activity 5

**Directions:** In each of the following sentences, circle the correct adverb.

1. That cloud is floating ( higher / highest ) than the others.

2. Simone types ( quicklier / more quickly ) than her mother.

3. When Matt behaved badly, his little brothers acted ( worse / worsely ).

4. Greg made milk shakes ( well / better ) than the ice cream shop.

5. Laura can draw dragons ( more / as ) well as any artist.

## TIP 6:  Make nouns and pronouns match.

You should also make sure that nouns and pronouns match. Remember, a noun is a person, place, or thing, and a pronoun is a word that takes the place of a noun (such as *it*).

Singular pronouns should take the place of singular nouns. Remember: Singular means one. A singular noun describes one thing, so a singular pronoun takes the place of one thing. For example, you can switch the singular noun *hat* with the singular pronoun *it*. Or, you can switch the singular noun *Wendy Parker* with the singular pronoun *she*.

**Plural nouns** describe more than one thing, so **plural pronouns** should take the place of more than one thing. You can switch the plural noun *hats* with the plural pronoun *them*. Or, you can switch the plural noun *the Parkers* with the plural pronoun *they*. Here are a few pronouns you might use in your writing:

| **Singular** | | | **Plural** | | |
|---|---|---|---|---|---|
| I | you | he/she/it | we | you | they |
| me | you | him/her/it | us | you | them |
| my | your | his/her/its | our | your | their |
| mine | yours | his/hers | ours | yours | theirs |

## Practice Activity 6

**Directions:** In the following sentences, circle the pronoun that matches the noun or nouns.

**Example:** Look at the blue jays! Aren't ( it / (they) ) lovely?

1. Bobby, Peter, and Cindy were hungry because ( he / they ) forgot to bring the picnic basket.

2. My brother and his best friend want to see a movie, but ( he / they ) don't have a ride.

3. Anne likes ( her / she ) six kittens.

4. Martin plays basketball with Carlos because ( he / them ) enjoys the sport.

5. The bakery sells ( its / their ) day-old bread for half price.

**TIP 7: Form regular and irregular plural nouns.**

Remember, a singular noun describes one thing while a plural noun describes more than one thing.

Usually you can make a singular noun into a plural noun by adding an *-s* or *-es* to the end of the noun. These are regular nouns.

| Singular | Plural | Singular | Plural |
|----------|--------|----------|--------|
| kite | kites | box | boxes |
| dog | dogs | peach | peaches |
| shoe | shoes | class | classes |

There are also **irregular nouns**. These nouns are changed from singular to plural in different ways.

**Some irregular nouns are spelled the same in both singular and plural forms.**

fish      deer      moose      sheep

**Some irregular nouns end in a consonant and a *-y*. To change into plural form, change the *-y* to an *-i* and add *-es*.**

| activity | activities | penny | pennies |
|----------|-----------|-------|---------|
| party | parties | baby | babies |
| spy | spies | puppy | puppies |

**Some irregular nouns end in *-f*. To change into plural form, change the *-f* to a *-v* and add *-es*.**

| calf | calves | wolf | wolves |
|------|--------|------|--------|
| leaf | leaves | wife | wives |

**Some irregular nouns contain two *o*'s. To change into plural form, change the *-oo-* to *-ee-*.**

foot      feet      goose      geese

**Some irregular nouns are changed into plural forms in different ways.**

ox      oxen      child      children

## TIP 8: Use different types of nouns.

You know a noun is a person, place, or thing. Nouns are also ideas, feelings, or thoughts. Be sure to use all different types of nouns, so that not all of your nouns are people or things. Using different nouns makes your writing more interesting.

Here are some nouns that are ideas or thoughts:

childhood     kindness     fairness     imagination     hope

## TIP 9: Adjectives use different endings.

You could go your whole life without ever using an adjective. But, just think how boring that would be! **Adjectives** are describing words. They describe nouns.

Adjectives describe people, places, and things.

- Sophia held her nose as she picked up her <u>stinky</u>, <u>old</u>, <u>red</u> sneakers.
- The <u>little</u> squirrel raced across the <u>green</u> lawn and up the <u>huge</u>, <u>old</u> tree.

Some adjectives compare two people, places, or things. These adjectives usually end in *-er* or begin with *more*.

- Broccoli is <u>healthier</u> than candy.
- Carlos thought the book was <u>more exciting</u> than the movie.

Other adjectives tell how something compares with many other people, places, and things. These adjectives usually end in *-est* or begin with *most*.

- My dog, Einstein, is the <u>smartest</u> dog I know.
- Lateesha thinks math is the <u>most interesting</u> class at school.

If the adjective ends in *-ly*, then you need to change the *-y* to an *-i* before adding *-er* or *-est*.

| | | |
|---|---|---|
| happy | happier | happiest |
| fast | faster | fastest |
| dry | drier | driest |
| loud | louder | loudest |

CCSs: L.3.1a, L.3.1g, L.3.3a

 **Practice Activity 7**

**Directions:** In the following sentences, circle the adjective that is correct.

1. My new bike is ( more faster / faster ) than my old bike.

2. Bell Witch Cave, in Adams, Tennessee, is one of the (most spooky / spookiest ) places in America.

3. Amara is the ( funniest / funnier ) person in the third grade.

4. What is the ( best / bestest ) way to drive to Boise, Idaho?

5. Jane is three inches ( tallest / taller ) than Jake.

6. Big Cypress Tree State Nature Area is one of the ( goodest / best ) places to go camping.

 **TIP 10: Find different ways to begin sentences.**

Read this paragraph.

> The three writers are lost in a forest. The forest has tall trees and creeping vines. The forest is dark.

All the sentences in this paragraph begin the same way: "The writers" or "The forest." What if *all* the sentences in a story started the same way? Boring!

1. The following two sentences begin the same way. Rewrite them on the following lines so that they start in different ways. You can change the order of the words or use different words in the sentences if you want to.

Steve rode his bicycle to the grocery store in the rain today.

Steve rode to the store to buy pepper and frozen peas.

_____

_____

_____

_____

_____

**TIP 11: Make sentences better by adding details.**

News reporters always ask six questions to make sure they get all the information they need about a story. They look for the answers to *Who? What? When? Why? Where?* and *How?* You can also use the words and phrases that answer these questions to make your sentences stronger.

Look at the following simple sentence:

Jesse practiced.

From this sentence, you only know the answer to *Who?* (*Jesse*) and *What?* (*practiced*). You probably want to know more.

2. Add on to the sentence above. Include information about the other three *W*s and the *H*. The first question has been answered for you.

Each sentence should be longer than the one before it.

Why?  *Jesse practiced for the track meet.*

Where? _____

_____

_____

When? _____

_____

_____

How? _____

_____

_____

_____

It's easy to write all different kinds of sentences—and it's a lot more fun than making them all the same. It helps your readers have more fun reading your writing, too!

**Practice Activity 8**

**Directions:** Choose the best words or phrases to complete the sentence. Each sentence should give as much detail as possible.

1. The captain flew the _____.

   A. plane                    C. big thing

   B. thing                    D. machine

2. The zookeeper loved to feed the _____.

   A. monkeys                  C. creatures

   B. animals                  D. living things

3. The puppy played with her _____.

   A. thing                    C. toy

   B. red thing                D. ball

4. The _____ ran around in a circle.

   A. animal                   C. horse

   B. creature                 D. thing

5. Today I _____ a Frisbee.

   A. played with              C. did something with

   B. threw                    D. held

 **TIP 12:  Use short, simple sentences.**

A **simple sentence** is a short sentence that contains a subject and verb. Look at the following examples of simple sentences.

Ben drew a picture of a robot.

He gave it to his brother.

There were no more frozen peas at the store.

Steve bought ice cream instead.

3.  Write three simple sentences of your own on the lines below.

_____

_____

_____

**➤ TIP 13:  Join two or more simple sentences together into a complex sentence.**

Writing can be boring if all the sentences are the same length. When writing, you can use simple and compound sentences. You just learned that a simple sentence is a short sentence that contains a subject and verb. A **compound sentence** is a sentence that joins two or more simple sentences.

To make a compound sentence, you can join two or more simple sentences together. You can do this by adding a comma (,) and a coordinating conjunction. A **comma** is a punctuation mark that tells the reader to pause. A **coordinating conjunction** is a word that joins two ideas together. The following words are conjunctions: *and*, *but*, *or*, *so*, and *since*.

Look at these two sentences.

> Molly plays the piano well.

> She is a terrible bowler.

You can turn these two simple sentences into one long sentence by adding a comma (,) and a conjunction.

Molly plays the piano well, <u>but</u> she is a terrible bowler.

4.  Add these simple sentences together.

The grocery store was crowded.

There were lots of shoppers.

_____

_____

_____

**Practice Activity 9**

**Directions:** Use coordinating conjunctions to put together each set of three sentences to make one or two new sentences.

1. Trisha is my sister.

   She is older than I am.

   She is my favorite babysitter.

   _____

   _____

   _____


2. I have a dog.

   She is a beagle.

   She does tricks if she's not sleeping.

   _____

   _____

   _____


3. Amanda is my best friend.

   We went to a movie last Saturday.

   We had lots of fun.

   _____

   _____

   _____

**TIP 14:  Use complex sentences to join a complete thought with an incomplete thought.**

In addition to writing simple and compound sentences, you can write complex sentences. A **complex sentence** has two parts: a complete thought and an incomplete thought. The complete thought is called the **independent clause**. It is the part of a sentence that can stand alone. Look at the example below:

> The man with one green shoe felt sick.

The incomplete thought is called the **dependent clause**. It is the part of a sentence that cannot stand alone. It makes sense only when it is with a complete thought. Look at the following dependent clause:

> after he ate the whole cake

That phrase does not make sense alone. We are left asking, "What happened after he ate the whole cake?"

To make a complex sentence, you can join a complete and an incomplete thought together. You can do this by using a subordinating conjunction. A **subordinating conjunction** is a word that joins dependent clauses to independent clauses. Here are some common subordinating conjunctions:

**Subordinating Conjunctions**

| | | | |
|---|---|---|---|
| after | even though | than | when |
| although | if | that | where |
| as | since | though | while |
| because | so that | unless | |
| before | | until | |

Sometimes you need to use a comma (,) to make a complex sentence. A **comma** is a punctuation mark that tells the reader to pause. If the incomplete thought (dependent clause) comes first, then you need to use a comma. If the incomplete thought (dependent clause) comes second, then you do not need to use a comma.

Here are some examples of complex sentences:

> After he ate the whole cake, the man with one green shoe felt sick.

> The man with one green shoe felt sick after he ate the whole cake.

**TIP 15: Remember that there are differences between written and spoken English.**

The way you speak on a day-to-day basis is different from the way you write. If you are speaking casually to your friends, you probably do not pay attention to *all* the details about English the way you need to when you write. Sometimes you might want to write down what you and others said. For example, Charmaine had a discussion with a doctor. She wants to write down parts of the discussion in an essay about medicine. This is part of Charmaine's chat with the doctor.

---

**Charmaine:** How many patients do you see each day?

**Doctor:** About 10. Sometimes more.

**Charmaine:** How long have you been working as a doctor?

**Doctor:** 25 years

**Charmaine:** What do you like about being a doctor?

**Doctor:** lots of things, hmm, helping people, seeing new babies, getting to know whole families

---

 **Practice Activity 10**

**Directions:** As you can see, parts of Charmaine's chat with the doctor are not complete sentences. They are missing nouns and verbs. Below, write the part of the discussion correctly using standard written English.

1. "25 years"

   _____

   _____

2. "lots of things, hmm, helping people, seeing new babies, getting to know whole families"

   _____

   _____

   _____

**Lesson Practice begins on the following page.**

**Directions:** This passage is about Tanya and her sled dogs. Read the passage. Then, answer Numbers 1 through 7.

# A Snowy Race

Tanya were behind in the race. She could see the other teams ahead of her. Tanya was in a dog race. "C'mon Rusty and Maroon!" she shouted to her dogs. *We will win this race!* Tanya thought to herself. Her dogs bolted and ran faster and faster. The sled whipped over the snowy hill. Tanya and her team of dogs had passed the other sleds. When she could see the red finish line, she knew they were going to win!

1. **Read this sentence from the story.**

   "Tanya were behind in the race."

   **Which of the following shows correct subject and verb agreement?**

   A. Tanyas were behind in the race.

   B. Tanyas was behind in the race.

   C. Tanya weres behind in the race.

   D. Tanya was behind in the race.

2. **Which of the following verbs from the story is in the future tense?**

   A. could see          C. will win

   B. shouted            D. had passed

3. **Which of the following is an adverb in the story?**

   A. faster

   B. snowy

   C. red

   D. team

4.   Which of the following is a subordinating conjunction in the  story?

 A.   ahead

 B.   herself

 C.   other

 D.   when

5.   Write down all the adjectives you find in the story.

 _____

 _____

 _____

6.   Write down all the pronouns you find in the story.

 _____

 _____

 _____

7.   Identify two simple sentences in the story. Write them here as a compound sentence.

 _____

 _____

 _____

# Lesson 20: Capitalization and Punctuation

my Sister left a note. for me but im, not, "sure what She meant" she! said meet me By the Flagpole down on brown street jacob. jackson has a new Game he says is quite neat cassie? will be there too im. not sure How to follow My sisters leTTer.

Can you figure out the writer's meaning? If the writer had used correct capitalization (capital letters) and punctuation, the meaning would be a lot clearer. If you don't use capital letters properly, your writing will be hard to read. When you are editing your writing, always check for capitalization.

## Capitalization

 **TIP 1: Capitalize proper nouns and other important words.**

Always capitalize . . .

- **the first word of each new sentence.**

  When does the bus leave? We better hurry or we might miss it.

- **people's names.**

  Bill Cosby       Lisa Simpson       Adam Sandler

  Lois Lowry       Charlie Brown       Mary Smith

- **titles before a name (but not after the name).**

  Prince Harry       Dr. Janet Jones       Mrs. Potter

  President Lincoln       Senator McCaskill       General Patton

  (but *Janet Jones, a doctor*, and *George Patton, a general*)

- **words used in place of a family member's name.**

  Mom       Granddad       Papa       Grandmother

  (Do *not* capitalize these names when used with such words as *our*, *my*, *his*, or *her*. Examples: *my mom, our granddad, his papa, her grandmother*.)

- **names of cities, states, countries, continents, nationalities, languages, and bodies of water.**

  Missouri       Ghana       Asia       Atlantic Ocean

  St. Louis       English       Spanish       Missouri River

- **days, months, and holidays. (Do not capitalize seasons.)**

  <u>W</u>ednesday, <u>O</u>ctober 31, is <u>H</u>alloween. <u>I</u>t's just one of autumn's special days.

- **brand names.**

  <u>D</u>annon    <u>T</u>ropicana    <u>C</u>heerios    <u>F</u>ord

- **titles of books, movies, and songs. (Do not capitalize words such as *of*, *and*, or *the* unless they are the first word of the title.)**

  *<u>C</u>harlotte's <u>W</u>eb*    *<u>T</u>arzan*    *<u>W</u>innie-the-<u>P</u>ooh*

  *<u>S</u>pring <u>C</u>omes to the <u>O</u>cean*    "<u>J</u>ingle <u>B</u>ells"

- **the pronoun *I*.**

  <u>I</u> heard the eye doctor say that <u>I</u> have perfect eyes.

- **the greeting and closing of a letter.**

  <u>D</u>ear <u>M</u>r. <u>R</u>eynolds,    <u>T</u>o <u>W</u>hom <u>I</u>t <u>M</u>ay <u>C</u>oncern,

  <u>S</u>incerely,    <u>F</u>rom,

- **in addresses (people's proper names, street names, cities, and states).**

  <u>W</u>eird <u>W</u>ild <u>S</u>lide <u>P</u>ark <u>C</u>ompany

  1234 <u>P</u>ark <u>St</u>.

  <u>P</u>arksville, <u>T</u>exas 77578

## Practice Activity 1

**Directions:** Rewrite each sentence, capitalizing where necessary. You may look back at the capitalization rules on pages 220 and 221 for help.

1.  my sister, tina, and i went to the mall on saturday.

    _____

    _____

2.  macy's will have its thanksgiving day parade on thursday, november 25.

    _____

    _____

# End punctuation

**End punctuation** tells your reader when one sentence stops and another sentence begins. End marks give your reader a chance to pause between sentences. The following tips to tell which kind of end punctuation to use.

 **TIP 2:  Use a question mark (?) at the end of every question.**

What did you name your new puppy?      What is on television tonight?

 **TIP 3:  Use an exclamation point (!) to show urgency or feelings.**

For expressing strong feelings, use an exclamation point (!). But don't overdo it. Save exclamation points for those times when you really need them.

Their attitude was so rude!      We won!      Don't look in that closet!

 **TIP 4:  Use a period (.) to end sentences that make a statement (give you information).**

Put a period at the end of statements that don't ask a question or show great feelings or excitement.

Walter learned to ice-skate before I did.

Ocelots are small, wild cats that look like leopards.

 ## Practice Activity 2

**Directions: Proofread** (correct) the following sentences. Place a period (.), a question mark (?), or an exclamation point (!) at the end of each sentence.

1. I enjoy reading a good book _____

2. What time does the play begin _____

3. The curtains are on fire _____

CCSs: L.3.2.b, L.3.2.c

# Commas

**Commas** (,) make the reader pause and "change gears," much like you would change speeds on a bicycle. The following tips discuss some of the rules for using commas.

 **TIP 5:** **Use commas *before* and *after* someone's name when you speak directly to them.**

Yoko, may I go to Taco Palace with you?

If I could draw like you, Latasha, I'd make my own valentines.

 **TIP 6:** **Use commas between a street address, city, and state when they are written on the same line. (Note: There is no comma between the state and ZIP code.)**

Mail this form to State Capitol Building, Jefferson City, MO 65101.

Lonnie moved to Silver Dollar City, 399 Indian Point Road, Branson, MO 65616.

 **TIP 7:** **Use commas *before* and *after* the year when it is used with a month and day.**

He bought the house on May 1, 2005, and moved in the following month.

The Cardinals won the pennant on October 21, 2008, before a sold-out crowd.

The *Titanic* sank on April 15, 1912.

**TIP 8:** **Use commas in the greeting and closing of a friendly letter.**

Dear Snow White, (Greeting)

Everyone misses you around the castle. They all wonder whether you are still as lovely as ever. I'm sending along a little present for your birthday—a basket of apples from the palace gardens. Enjoy!

Your loving stepmother, (Closing)

Zelda

 **TIP 9:** **Use commas with quotation marks (" ") when showing people speaking.**

"The zoo is fun," Todd said.      Miri yelled, "Happy birthday, Marge!"

# Apostrophes

**Apostrophes** are little signals (') used for two things. They show where letters are missing in contractions (*was* + *not* = *wasn't*). They also show ownership when used with nouns (*Bill's hat*). The following tips review when to use an apostrophe.

 **TIP 10:** **Use an apostrophe (') to show where letters are missing in a contraction.**

A **contraction** combines two words into one. An apostrophe takes the place of a letter or letters that drop out of the new word.

you + will = you'll

In the contraction above, the apostrophe takes the place of the missing *wi* in the word *will*.

CCS: L.3.2c

 **TIP 11: Use an apostrophe (') to show ownership.**

Read the following sentences.

<u>The kite belonging to Marlene</u> was difficult to build.

<u>Marlene's kite</u> was difficult to build.

Which sentence is easier to read? In the second sentence, the 's added to *Marlene* tells us who the owner is. By understanding apostrophes, you can make nouns show ownership by adding 's.

# Quotation Marks

When people talk to each other about something, they are having a conversation. You probably have conversations with your friends every day. Written conversations can be very hard to understand if they aren't written in a certain way.

**Quotation marks (" ")** show spoken words. They may also be used around important words or phrases, such as titles of stories, songs, and poems. Quotation marks always come in pairs.

 **TIP 12: Use quotation marks (" ") around the words people say.**

"Watch me hit the ball," Ashley said.

 **TIP 13: Put a comma inside the quotation marks at the end of a person's words.**

"Don't blame me," Jenny said.

 **TIP 14: Put end punctuation inside the quotation marks, too.**

Abby replied, "I have to blame someone."

**Practice Activity 3**

**Directions:** Put quotation marks around the spoken words in the following sentences.

1. Tanya said, I don't want to go to bed until 11:00.

2. I'm going to watch *American Idol*, Alexis said.

3. Aunt Lila said, Be home by lunchtime.

4. No, thank you, she replied, I don't think I'd like tuna fish ice cream.

5. Hey, Josh! Cheri yelled. I scored two goals in today's game.

 **TIP 15:** **Use quotation marks to show titles of stories, songs, and poems.**

Quotation marks go at the beginning and end of some titles. (Not every title takes quotation marks. Books and movies use *italic print* or <u>underlining</u> instead.) Stories, articles, songs, and poems use quotation marks.

Here are some examples.

My favorite bedtime story is "Goldilocks and the Three Bears."

"The Farmer in the Dell" is a song that came from Germany 200 years ago.

Most children know the poem "Hickory Dickory Dock" by heart.

Put quotation marks where needed in the following sentences.

1. The funniest poem I know is The Spider and the Fly.

2. Janet read Jack and the Beanstalk from a storybook.

**Lesson Practice begins on the following page.**

**Directions:** This passage is about different pets. Read the passage. Then answer Numbers 1 through 8.

# *Pets*

*by Ariana Vásquez*

Randy and Melissa live on a small farm in the country. Their farm is outside brockport, new york. Randy and Melissa each have a pet. Randy has a 12-year-old pony named Bud. Melissa has a cat named Lulu.

Randy has a pony named Bud.

Randy takes care of Bud? He feeds Bud in his stall in the barn. He takes Bud out in the pasture to eat grass and get exercise. Sometimes, Randy puts on a saddle and rides Bud. Bud will let Randy ride him. Nobody else can ride, Bud, however.

It doesn't bother Melissa that she can't ride Bud. Thats because she has Lulu. Lulu is part Siamese. She has a tan body with black around her face, legs, and tail. Lulu also has beautiful blue eyes. When Melissa comes home from school, Lulu goes up to her and meows. Lulu then rubs her back against Melissas legs. Melissa picks up Lulu and pets her. Lulu purrs like a car engine Then Melissa feeds Lulu, and they have fun together.

Randy wants another pet. He keeps asking his mom, "Can I have a snake?" Randy wants a special kind of snake. "It's called a corn snake, Mom."

Snakes can bite says Mom

"The pet store guy says these snakes are gentle. All I need is a large glass case with a box inside where the snake can hide. Corn snakes are beautiful. They is easy to keep. What do you say?"

Mom thinks for a minute! "How about we get one for your birthday? But I want you to teach me how to ride Bud!"

"It's a deal, Mom."

1.  **Which sentence shows correct punctuation?**

    A.  Randy takes care of Bud?

    B.  Nobody else can ride, Bud, however.

    C.  Mom thinks for a minute!

    D.  "It's a deal, Mom."

2.  **Read this sentence from the story.**

    Lulu purrs like a car engine

    **What punctuation mark should be added to this sentence?**

    A.  .                           C.  ?

    B.  !                           D.  ,

3.  **Read this sentence from the story.**

    Their farm is outside brockport, new york.

    **This sentence is incorrectly capitalized. Which of the following sentences shows correct capitalization?**

    A.  Their farm is outside Brockport, new york.

    B.  Their farm is outside Brockport, New York.

    C.  Their farm is outside brockport, New York.

    D.  Their farm is outside Brockport, New york.

4.  **Read this sentence from the story.**

    Thats because she has Lulu.

    **This sentence is incorrectly punctuated. Which of the following sentences shows correct punctuation?**

    A.  That's because she has Lulu.

    B.  That'is because she has Lulu.

    C.  That's' because she has Lulu.

    D.  Thats' because she has Lulu.

5. **Read this sentence from the story.**

   Snakes can bite says Mom

   **This sentence is missing punctuation. Rewrite the sentence on the lines below. Add correct punctuation.**

   _____

   _____

6. **Read this sentence from the story.**

   Lulu then rubs her back against Melissas legs.

   **This sentence is missing punctuation. Rewrite the sentence on the lines below. Add correct punctuation.**

   _____

   _____

7. **It looks like Randy will be getting another pet. How will Melissa most likely react to this news? Use details from the story in your answer. Be sure to use correct punctuation.**

   _____

   _____

   _____

   _____

   _____

   _____

8.  Here is a paragraph a student wrote about her favorite movie. The paragraph has some mistakes in punctuation. Some sentences may have no mistakes. There are no mistakes in spelling.

    Read the paragraph, and find the mistakes. Circle each mistake in the paragraph. On the lines below, write the revised paragraph.

    My favorite story is The Little Mermaid. It tells about a mermaid named Ariel. She has a beautiful voice. I love when she sings Part of Your World. Ariel falls in love with a human prince. A witch turns her into a person, but she takes Ariels voice. Ariel has help from her friends Flounder Sebastian and Scuttle. In the end, Ariel marries the prince. Yay?

_____

_____

_____

_____

_____

CCS: L.3.2f

# Lesson 21: Spelling Tools

Who thought of putting a *c* in *place* instead of an *s*? Or a *g* in *gem* instead of a *j*? Sometimes it seems that the spelling of our language doesn't make sense. English has thousands of words. Some are easy to spell. Others take a while to learn how to spell correctly. But easy or hard, most English words follow some simple rules that can help you spell them.

In this lesson, you will learn some common spelling patterns. Understanding these patterns will help you a lot in your writing.

 **TIP 1:  Use syllable patterns.**

In Lesson 2, you learned that a **syllable** is a word part that makes its own sound. Syllables can be made up of a vowel or vowels with consonants. Many words in the English language follow common syllable patterns. You can use these syllable patterns to correctly spell words.

Here are a few syllable patterns:

| consonant-vowel-consonant (CVC) | consonant-vowel-consonant-*e* (CVCe) | consonant-vowel-vowel-consonant (CVVC) |
|---|---|---|
| sat | bike | grain |
| hat | lake | need |
| bit | pine | shout |
| pup | rose | weak |

**Practice Activity 1**

**Directions:** In the sentences that follow, circle the incorrectly spelled word. Then spell the word correctly. Use what you know about syllable patterns to help you. The first one has been done for you.

1. The cook put the fresh corn into the (paht) to boil in water.

   __pot_____

2. My throt feels sore, so I think I'm getting a cold.

   _____

3. Penguins lik to eat a lot of fish.

   _____

 **TIP 2:  Remember word families.**

**Word families** are groups of words that are spelled alike. When you learn a new word, try to think of another word that it is spelled like. This will help you remember how to spell when you are sounding out words in your head. Look at the word families on the following page.

CCS: L.3.2f

| the "ee" family | the "oa" family | the "ch" family |
|---|---|---|
| freeze | float | chilly |
| sneeze | boat | child |
| meet | foam | chicken |
| sheet | moan | chuckle |

Other word families include *ck*, *sh*, *rr*, *fr*, *ing*, *ai*, *ou*, and *st*.

Now it's your turn. On the lines below, list three words in the *-oo-* family.
(**Example:** *b<u>oo</u>k*)

_____    _____    _____

**Practice Activity 2**

**Directions:** In the table below, fill in each space with a word from the same word family as the example. Use the picture clues to help you.

## Word Patterns Table

| | |
|---|---|
| **sh**irt | _____ |
| **ch**eese | _____ |
| wa**sp** | _____ |
| **bee**hive | _____ |
| fl**oa**t | _____ |
| m**ou**th | _____ |

CCS: L.3.2f

 **TIP 3: Remember the rules for forming plurals.**

For most words, add -*s* to form the plural:

candle + s = candle<u>s</u>

day + s = day<u>s</u>

truck + s = truck<u>s</u>

For words ending in *s*, *ss*, *ch*, or *x*, add -*es*:

pass + es = pass<u>es</u>

beach + es = beach<u>es</u>

tax + es = tax<u>es</u>

For words ending in a consonant plus *y*, change the *y* to *i* and add -*es*:

city → cit + i + es = cities

pony → pon + i + es = ponies

 **Practice Activity 3**

**Directions:** Write the plural form of each word.

|  | **Singular** | **Plural** |
|---|---|---|
| **Example:** | cup | cups |
| 1. | elephant | |
| 2. | family | |
| 3. | movie | |
| 4. | canary | |
| 5. | watch | |

**Practice Activity 4**

**Directions:** Write the correct spelling of each misspelled word on the line below it.

1. Can money really grow on *treees*?

   _____

2. Emiliano has a hundred *cares* in his toy car collection.

   _____

3. I wonder how many *storys* I could write in one day.

   _____

4. Terry *enjoies* fishing in the lake behind his grandma's cabin.

   _____

5. The green knight stood on the hill sharpening his three *axs*.

   _____

 **TIP 4: Suffixes can sometimes cause spelling problems.**

You learned in Lesson 2 that you can add letters to the end of a word to change its meaning. The letters that are added are called **suffixes**. The next few pages will remind you of a few rules for adding suffixes.

If a word ends with a consonant followed by *y*, change the *y* to an *i* before adding the suffix:

   hungry + ly = hungr<u>il</u>y

If a word ends with a vowel followed by *y*, do NOT change the *y* to an *i*:

   stay + ed = stay<u>ed</u>

For suffixes beginning with *i* (such as *-ing*), do NOT change the *y*:

   cry + ing = cry<u>ing</u>

CCSs: L.3.2e, L.3.2f

 ## Practice Activity 5

**Directions:** Add the suffixes to the following words.

1. lazy + ly = _____

2. spy + ed = _____

 ## Practice Activity 6

**Directions:** Correct the spelling of each misspelled word on the lines below.

1. The clown was *triing* hard to make us laugh.

_____

2. Siri *studyed* for the history test.

_____

3. The dog freed itself *easyly* from the leash.

_____

 **TIP 5: Be careful about the *e* when adding suffixes.**

You can add suffixes to words that end in *e*. Sometimes you will keep the *e*, and other times you want to get rid of the *e*.

Here are some examples:

If the suffix begins with a vowel (*-ed*, *-er*, *-ing*), drop the silent *e* at the end of the word before adding the suffix:

bake + ing = bak<u>ing</u>

If the suffix begins with a consonant (*-ly*, *-ful*), keep the silent *e*:

lone + ly = lonel<u>y</u>

Some words are exceptions to this spelling rule, such as the following:

true + ly = tru<u>ly</u>      whole + ly = wholl<u>y</u>

**Practice Activity 7**

**Directions:** Add the suffixes to the following words.

1. ashame + ed = _____

2. chose + en = _____

3. doze + ing = _____

4. dance + ed = _____

5. pure + ly = _____

6. care + less = _____

7. owe + ed = _____

 **Practice Activity 8**

**Directions:** Write the correct spelling of each misspelled word on the line below it.

1. George keeps *closeing* the door too fast.

_____

2. The weather reporter said that rain is *likly*.

_____

3. Tara is *hopful* that she will find her lost lizard.

_____

4. My dog is *chaseing* its tail again.

_____

CCS: L.3.2f

 **TIP 6: Learn how to make contractions.**

As you learned in Lesson 20, a **contraction** is two words that are squeezed together into one word with some of the letters taken out. An apostrophe (') takes the place of the missing letter or letters.

Look at the following examples of contractions:

can + not = **can't** (The apostrophe takes the place of the letters *no*.)

you + will = **you'll** (The apostrophe takes the place of the letters *wi*.)

they + have = **they've** (The apostrophe takes the place of the letters *ha*.)

it + is = **it's** (The apostrophe takes the place of the letter *i*.)

we + are = **we're** (The apostrophe takes the place of the letter *a*.)

 **Practice Activity 9**

**Directions:** Make the following words into contractions. You may look back at the examples to help you.

1. are + not = _____

2. he + will = _____

3. I + have = _____

4. she + is = _____

5. they + are = _____

**TIP 7:  Split up compound words into smaller words.**

A **compound word** is a word made of two or more smaller words. An example of a compound word is *rowboat*. Think about the smaller words that make up the whole word. Smaller words that make up *rowboat* are *row* and *boat*. This will make spelling easier.

 **Practice Activity 10**

**Directions:** Look at the following compound words. Then split each compound word into its smaller words.

**Example:** watermelon = _water + melon_____

1.  typewriter = _____

2.  rattlesnake = _____

3.  peppermint = _____

4.  earthquake = _____

5.  basketball = _____

CCS: L.3.2e

 ## TIP 8: Correctly spell common words.

There are a lot of words you probably use all the time. Some of these words you might spell correctly often. Others you might have trouble spelling. Try to memorize the correct spelling of words you use all the time.

Here is a list of words that you probably use often and should learn how to spell correctly:

| | | |
|---|---|---|
| about | believe | better |
| bring | carry | clean |
| cut | difficult | done |
| draw | drink | easy |
| eight | friendly | hold |
| hurt | if | keep |
| kind | laugh | light |
| much | myself | never |
| only | own | pick |
| seven | shall | show |
| six | start | today |
| through | together | warm |

**TIP 9:** **Homophones are words that sound alike but are spelled differently and mean different things.**

Here are a few of these tricky words:

| | |
|---|---|
| **by** | School is over **by** June. |
| **bye** | Say good-**bye** to tests. |
| **buy** | Let's rush out to **buy** swimsuits for the summer. |
| **dear** | I began my letter with "**Dear** Silvia." |
| **deer** | I wrote about seeing the **deer** in the forest. |
| **it's** (it is) | **It's** true that Ellen has a lion. |
| **its** | Last night, we could hear **its** roars from her room. |
| | (Note: There is no such word as *its'*.) |
| **write** | Jacob sits down to **write** a scary story. |
| **right** | He doesn't notice the monster sitting to his **right**. |
| **road** | Frank flew down the **road** in search of excitement. |
| **rode** | He **rode** his bike until he reached the ice cream truck. |
| **their** | Chelsea and Liz brought **their** diaries to school. |
| **they're** (they are) | **They're** going to read them during recess. |
| **there** | They left them **there** on the playground. |
| **to** | Are you going **to** the parade? |
| **two** | **Two** of our friends will be in the marching band. |
| **too** | We will see a baton twirler, **too**. |
| **wade** | I like to **wade** in the water when I go fishing. |
| **weighed** | I once caught a fish that **weighed** 100 pounds. |
| **where** | **Where** are you going? |
| **wear** | You can't **wear** a swimsuit to the shopping mall! |
| **would** | **Would** you please help Mario? |
| **wood** | He is chopping some **wood** for the campfire. |

CCSs: L.3.2e, L.3.2g

 ## Practice Activity 11

**Directions:** Circle the word in parentheses ( ) that best fits each sentence.

1. Ursula decided to ( by / bye / buy ) popsicles and pears at the store.

2. How long does it take Earth ( to / too / two ) go around the sun?

3. If you were a girl living in the nineteenth century, you might ( where / wear ) long, heavy dresses.

4. Jeff and Andy took ( there / their / they're ) model airplanes to the park.

5. ( Its / It's ) important to know which way is the ( write / right ) way to travel on a one-way street.

## TIP 10: Use a dictionary to check and correct spelling.

When you are writing, you can use a dictionary to check your spelling. You can find words you can't remember how to spell, words that are new, or words that you know you spelled incorrectly.

Consider this example of a student's paragraph that contains incorrectly used words.

> My brother and I went <u>too</u> the carnival. I wanted to go on the merry-go-round. My brother wanted to go <u>two</u>. So, I bought <u>to</u> tickets. We had a great time! The student used the dictionary to choose the correct word.

**to – tyke   31**

**to**, *prep* 1. In the direction of 2. About

**toll**, *n.* 1. A fee or a charge *v.* 1. To make a sound 2. To charge a fee

**too**, *adv.* 1. Also 2. Very

**two**, *n.* 1. A number (2) 2. Two units of something

## ✎ Practice Activity 12

**Directions:** For each of the following words, write a sentence that uses the word correctly. You may use a dictionary to look up any words you are unsure of.

1. be _____

   bee _____


2. meet _____

   meat _____


3. close _____

   clothes _____


4. dew _____

   do _____

   due _____

**Directions:** For each of the following words, circle the incorrectly used word or words. Then rewrite the sentence with the correct word. You may use a dictionary to look up the words.

5. The carrier pigeon was cent with a message tied to it's leg.

   _____

   _____

6. Do you no what time the movie starts tonight?

   _____

   _____

### Lesson Practice begins on the following page.

**Directions:** This passage is about different pets. Read the passage. Then answer Numbers 1 through 8.

# *A Real Treat*

Do you like to make your own treats? If so, you probably no you need to be safe in the kitchen. If you use the stove or oven, or need to cutt anything with a knife, then you definitely need an adult to help!

But sometimes you might want to make something on your own to eat or to surprise your family. But it can be hard to find a recipe for a treat that you can make on your own. Here is a recipe you can make on your own.

---

**Strawberry-Banana Cream Pie**

1 store-bought graham cracker pie crust

1 package of whipped cream

3 cups milk

2 packags of instant banana pudding mix

1 small jar of strawberry jam

Fresh strawberries

---

Step 1.  In a large bowl, mix the milk and instant pudding mix. Put in the refrigerator.

Step 2.  Take out the pie crust. Gently scoop several spoonfuls of strawberry jam into the bottom of the pie crust. Use the back of the spoon to spread the jam across the bottom of the pie crust.

Step 3.  Pour the pudding over the jam in the pie crust.

Step 4.  Use a spoon to spread whipped cream over the pudding.

Step 5.  Cover the top with fresh strawberrys. Make sure the entire top is covered!

Step 6.  Put in the refrigerator for about an hour.

1.  **Read this sentence from the passage.**

    If so, you probably no you need to be safe in the kitchen.

    **Which word is incorrectly used in this sentence?**

    A.  probably          C.  need

    B.  no               D.  to

2.  **Read this sentence from the passage.**

    If you use the stove or oven, or need to cutt anything with a knife, then
    you definitely need an adult to help!

    **This sentence contains a spelling mistake. Which of the following shows this
    sentence correctly spelled?**

    A.  If you use the stove or oven, or need to cut anything with a knife, then you
        definitely need an adult to help!

    B.  If you use the stove or oven, or need to cutt anything with a nife, then you
        definitely need an adult to help!

    C.  If you us the stove or oven, or nead to cut anything with a knife, then you
        definitely need an adult to help!

    D.  If you use the stove or oven, or need to cute anything with a knife, then you
        definitely need an adult to help!

3.  **Which of the following is a compound word in the passage?**

    A.  definitely          C.  pudding

    B.  surprise            D.  sometimes

4.  **Read this sentence from the passage.**

    Here is a recipe you can make on your own.

    **Which of the following shows the correct contraction of "Here is?"**

    A.  Here's          C.  Here'is

    B.  Here's'         D.  Heres

5.  **Read this line from the recipe.**

    2 packags of instant banana pudding mix

    **This line contains a misspelled word. Rewrite the line on the lines.**

    **Correct the misspelled word.**

    _____

    _____

    _____

6.  **Read this sentence from the recipe.**

    Gentely scoop several spoonfuls of strawberry jam into the bottom of the
    pie crust.

    **This sentence contains a misspelled word. Rewrite the sentence on the lines.**

    **Correct the misspelled word.**

    _____

    _____

    _____

7.  **Read this sentence from the recipe.**

    Cover the top with fresh strawberrys.

    **This sentence contains a misspelled word. Rewrite the sentence on the lines.**

    **Correct the misspelled word.**

    _____

    _____

    _____

8.  Here is a paragraph a student wrote about his favorite hobby. The paragraph has 11 spelling mistakes. Some sentences may have no mistakes. There are no mistakes in punctuation.

    Read the paragraph and find the mistakes. Circle each mistake in the paragraph. On the lines below, write the revised paragraph.

---

Some kids get board on rainey afternoons. But I don'ot! I love those days because I no I have tim to do one of my favorite things. I like to build my own musical instruments! I use stuff around the hoose. I put buttones or dried corn into an empty milk jug to mak a shaker. I use empty jars and cans and tap them with spoons to mak a drum. To mak a little guitar, I string many different-sized rubber bands around a bowl. Then, I pluck the rubber bands to mak music!

---

_____

_____

_____

_____

_____

_____

_____

_____

_____

# Listening and Speaking

There are many times when you need to listen to and speak with others. You might need to listen to your teacher, your parent, a politician, or a group leader. You might talk in front of others when giving a speech or report. Also, there are lots of times when you talk with a group, such as a group of friends, students, teammates, and other people.

In this unit, you'll learn how to be an active listener and successful speaker. As you listen, you can use many different tools to understand and remember what you are hearing. You can also use special tools to prepare to give a speech and to be a helpful part of a successful discussion.

## In This Unit

Listen Up!

Discuss It!

Speaking Loudly and Clearly

# Lesson 22: Listen Up!

It is important to listen. Your friends tell you what food to bring to a party, your science teacher tells you how to do an experiment, the crossing guard tells you to stand on the street corner—these are examples of when it is important to listen.

This girl is being a careful listener.

Sometimes you will listen to a story or passage. Your teacher might read to you in school for fun, to give you information, or to give instructions during a test. Often, after listening, you will be asked to respond to what you heard. You might be asked to remember details from what you heard or to figure out the main idea. So, it is very important that you practice being a good listener.

Here's a story that shows why it's important to be a good listener.

---

Kyra was watching TV when the phone rang. Kyra moaned. *Why does the phone always ring when I'm trying to watch TV?* she thought.

"Hello?"

"Is Rob there?" Rob was Kyra's older brother.

"No," Kyra said. She made a face. Her brother's friends ALWAYS called.

"Would you give him a message?"

"I guess so," Kyra said, wishing he'd hurry up.

"Write this down. It's important. Practice is at 5:30 tomorrow, not 6:30."

"Okay," Kyra said. She was only half-listening, and she didn't write anything down. Her favorite show was on. Besides, she had a pretty good memory.

"Thanks! Don't forget to give him the message."

"I won't. Bye," Kyra said. Her eyes stayed glued to the TV.

Later, when Rob came home, he asked, "Any calls?"

Kyra didn't look up from the TV. "Your friend called. He said practice is at *6:30* tomorrow," she said. "*I think* that's what he said," she added.

---

CCS: SL.3.2

 **TIP 1: The first time the story is read to you, listen and enjoy.**

The first time you hear the passage, just sit back, relax, and listen. Enjoy the story being read to you. Don't interrupt the reader.

 **TIP 2: Listen for the main idea and important details.**

The second time the story is read, focus on listening. Imagine the characters or people in the story and the details. Try not to think about anything but the story. Close your eyes, if it helps.

As you listen, ask yourself these questions:

- Am I hearing details that are important to the story or passage?

- What is the main message in the story or passage?

By focusing on listening, you'll be better able to remember and understand the details and main idea in the passage.

 **TIP 3: Connect what you hear to what you see.**

Sometimes you will be able to look at charts, diagrams, graphs, and pictures while listening to a reading. These charts and pictures often hold helpful information, or they show the information in the passage in a clear way.

If you are listening to a reading that also has charts or pictures, you need to focus on listening while looking at the charts or pictures. How do you know when to listen or when to listen *and* look at the pictures? Always focus on listening. If the story or passage describes details in the chart or picture, then take a moment to look at it. The person reading might also give you a moment to just look at the pictures. But when the reader starts to read again or moves onto new information, you want to be focused completely on listening. Remember, always listen!

 **TIP 4: When the story is read the second time, take notes.**

The second time the story is read, write down notes. **Notes** are short phrases and sentences that help remind you about parts of the story later on. Your notes should not be full sentences. They can just be a few words. You want your notes to be short so that you can write them while still listening. When taking notes, quickly write down a few words about the main idea. Or write down the most important details in the story. Your notes will help you remember the story.

 **TIP 5: Don't try to write down everything.**

If you write down too many notes, you may not listen as well. Instead, write down only the things you think are most important to the story.

**251**

**TIP 6: When the story is read the second time, ask questions about what you have heard.**

To be a good listener, you actually need to do a lot! As you listen the second time, you can ask yourself different questions to help yourself better understand what you are hearing. As you listen, you can write your questions in your notes.

You can ask yourself questions about the passage, such as:

- What is the main event or action happening?
- Who is doing the action?
- What is the order of events?
- Where are the events happening?
- What is the reason the author wrote the passage?
- What are the most important details?
- What is the main idea?

What are some other questions you can think of to ask yourself as you listen?

_____

_____

_____

You can also ask yourself questions about your understanding of what you are listening to, such as:

- Do I understand the passage?
- Do I ever get confused? If so, when?
- Is there anything I'm curious about?
- Does this remind me of any personal experience?
- Do I know anything about the topic?

What are some other questions you can ask yourself about your understanding?

_____

_____

_____

CCSs: SL.3.2, SL.3.3, SL.3.4

 **TIP 7:** **Support your answers to questions with details from the passage or presentation.**

Once you've finished listening to the passage, you will often be asked questions about the passage. You will not have the passage to look at to answer these questions. To answer these questions, use your notes!

- You might be asked to identify details from the passage. Even if you remember the answer, you should check your notes to be sure. Also, you can use the details in your notes to support your answer.

- You might be asked to share your thoughts or opinions about something in the passage. Write your thoughts or opinions to answer the question. But be sure to support your response with details from the passage. You can look for details in your notes.

- You might be asked to share from your personal experiences. Your personal experiences are a great source of information. But when responding to questions about a passage, always show how your personal experiences connect to the passage. That means you need to use details from the passage that support your personal experiences. You can use your notes for these details, too.

**Lesson Practice begins on the following page.**

# Listening

You are going to listen to a passage called "Little Cities Under the Ground." Then you will answer some questions to show how well you understood the passage as well as the picture on page 255.

You will listen to the passage twice. The first time you hear the passage, listen carefully but do not take notes. As you listen to the passage the second time, you may want to take notes.

Use the space on the next page for your notes. You may use these notes to answer the questions that follow.

## As You Listen

✔ **Remember to:**

☐ listen to and enjoy the story the first time it is read.

☐ listen for the main idea and important details the second time the story is read.

☐ take short notes the second time the story is read.

☐ connect what you hear to the picture you see.

☐ ask yourself questions as you listen.

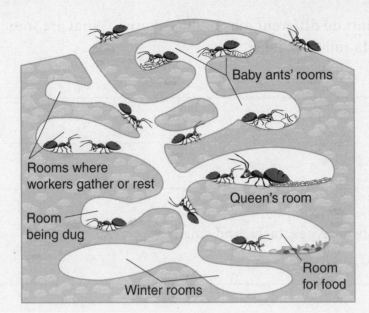

Baby ants' rooms

Rooms where workers gather or rest

Room being dug

Queen's room

Winter rooms

Room for food

**Directions:** Take notes in the space below. On the next page, you will answer questions about the passage and the art you see on this page.

_____

_____

_____

_____

_____

_____

_____

_____

_____

_____

1. Different ants do different jobs in the colonies. What are some of the different types of ants and their jobs?

   _____

   _____

   _____

2. How do ants hear, see, taste, and smell?

   _____

   _____

   _____

3. What might be a place on Earth that ants do not live? Use details from the passage to support your answer.

   _____

   _____

4. The diagram shows different rooms in an ant colony. What rooms would a worker ant be in, and what would the worker ant do in those rooms?

   _____

   _____

   _____

CCS: SL.3.1b

# Lesson 23: Discuss It!

In school, you probably discuss things differently than when you are simply talking with friends. During school discussions, you probably follow certain rules. You probably take turns, don't interrupt, and talk to reach a certain goal or finish a project. Your teacher might lead the discussion, ask questions, or tell students when to speak.

Sometimes, in school, you discuss something one-on-one with a partner, with the whole class, or with a discussion group. In a **discussion group**, a group of students talk about a topic in an organized way. The group talks in order to answer questions or complete a project. While a teacher might help with a discussion group, usually you and the other students in the group need to make sure to follow discussion rules together.

## TIP 1: Be respectful.

Before beginning a discussion group, your class might come up with a list of rules to follow. Or your teacher will give you a set of rules to follow.

Your teacher and your class might agree on rules, such as these:

- Take turns speaking. (Speak one at a time.)
- For each turn, take only a few moments to share so everyone has a chance.
- Do not interrupt another speaker; listen to others with care.
- If you disagree with anyone, say so in a respectful way. Talk about the other student's ideas or opinions. Do not talk about the other student.
- Talk in a regular voice. (Do not yell, shout, or whisper.)
- Remember to stay on topic.

What is another rule you could add to the list of discussion group rules?

_____

_____

What is a rule you might have a hard time following? How can you help make sure you follow that rule?

_____

_____

## TIP 2: Be prepared.

Before beginning a discussion, be sure you are prepared. You should complete any work about the topic beforehand, and bring any supplies you'll need.

For example, be sure you have already:

- read any texts you are to discuss.

- studied any texts or topics you are to discuss.

Also, bring with you:

- any books or materials you want to discuss.

- paper and pencil to take notes.

## TIP 3: Carry out your role in the discussion group.

The members of a discussion group have very important roles and responsibilities. During a discussion, it's important that all members are respectful of each other, stay on topic, and follow the discussion rules. Each member of a discussion group can have a different role and complete specific tasks so that the group stays organized and is successful. These are some discussion group roles:

| Role | Tasks |
|------|-------|
| **Discussion Leader** | Leads the discussion; keeps everyone on topic; asks questions. |
| **Recorder** | Takes clear and organized notes. |
| **Timekeeper** | Keeps time and helps keep the discussion moving on schedule. |
| **Checker** | Makes sure group members understand the ideas discussed. |
| **Summarizer** | Shares the group's ideas and conclusions with the class. |

It is very important that all group members work to complete their roles. No member should do all the tasks in a group. Each member should stick to the tasks of his or her role.

CCSs: SL.3.1b, SL.3.1c, SL.3.1d, SL.3.2, SL.3.4

## TIP 4: Ask questions about the discussion.

When you are part of a discussion group, ask questions. This can help you accomplish many things.

By asking questions, you can:

- show curiosity about what your group members think.
- show curiosity about your group's topic.
- help your group stay focused.
- respond to what your group members say.

## TIP 5: Add to the discussion by sharing and connecting ideas.

When you are part of a discussion group, share your thoughts and ideas. You can share facts, details, experiences you've had, books you've read, or other things. Just be sure to share ideas that are connected to the topic and connected to what other group members have said. By staying connected, you know you are helping your group be successful. Talking about other topics can distract your group.

When you share your thoughts and ideas, try to build on what other members say. You can name the group member and what he or she said, such as:

- *Mark said this and I agree because . . .*
- *Linda said this and it made me think of . . .*

## TIP 6: Think about what you learned from the discussion.

After you've completed the discussion, think about what you learned. Ask yourself if your opinions or feelings have changed.

- Do you think or feel differently about the topic now?
- How did your thoughts, feelings, and opinions change?
- Do you know more about the topic now? If so, what did you learn?

## Practice Activity

**Directions:** A group of students are in a discussion group. The topic is "What is the best school trip?" Read what students said and asked. Then draw a line through those things that are not focused on the topic.

---

**Tabby:** I think the best school trip is one that is fun and teaches us something.

**Marco:** What kind of school trips do that?

**Becky:** I think going to museums and zoos are fun and teach us something. What do you all think?

**Franco:** My family and I went on a camping trip last summer, and that was fun.

**Tabby:** I think zoos are also fun and teach us something.

**Marco:** I think so, too. So, Tabby, Becky, and I all think zoos are fun and teach us something. Franco, what do you think?

**Franco:** I think it's fun when we have a half day of school.

---

1. What is a question you could ask to build on what the members have said?

   _____

2. What is something you could say to build on what any of the members have said?

   _____

## Lesson Practice begins on the following page.

**Directions:** Read the following article about the rules that bicycle makers must follow when building bikes to sell and ways to stay safe while riding your bicycle. Then answer Numbers 1 through 3.

# Bicycle Safety Rules

Bicycles made in the United States must follow safety rules. Every bicycle must have reflectors on the front and back. They must also have reflectors in the wheel spokes. Reflectors are special pieces of plastic that allow the bike to be seen in the dark. The tires and brakes are inspected at the factory before the bicycles are shipped to stores.

Once you become the owner of a bicycle, it is your job to make sure that broken reflectors are replaced and that brakes work properly. You must also make sure that the air pressure in the tires is the same as that printed on the side of the tire.

Most states don't require that your bicycle have a bell or a horn. However, having a bell or horn on your bicycle can help keep you safe. By ringing a bell or honking a horn, you can warn others of your bicycle's approach.

Bicycle riders must follow all traffic laws if they ride on public streets or roads. For example, bike riders must use hand signals to show when they are slowing, turning, or stopping.

It is also important to wear a helmet when you ride your bicycle. Even the best bicycle riders get into accidents and fall off of their bicycles. The best way to keep from getting a serious injury is to wear a helmet.

## Bicycle Safety Rules

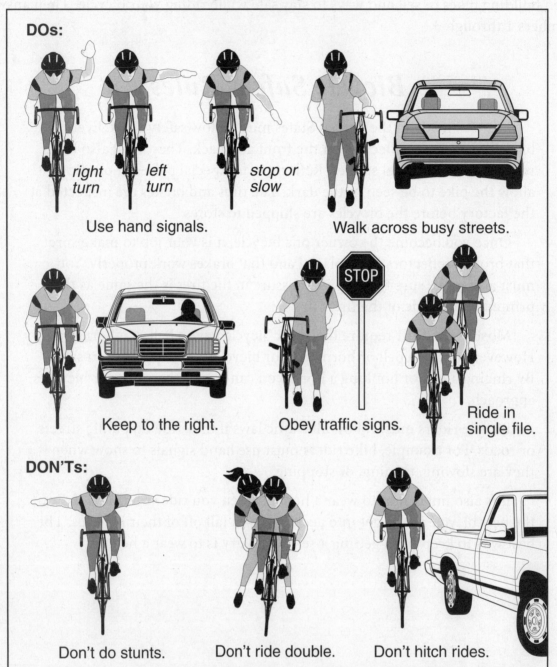

**DOs:**

right turn    left turn    stop or slow

Use hand signals.

Walk across busy streets.

Keep to the right.

Obey traffic signs.

Ride in single file.

**DON'Ts:**

Don't do stunts.

Don't ride double.

Don't hitch rides.

## Discussion Questions

1.  Do bicycle safety rules help bicycle riders or car drivers more? Why?

    _____

    _____

    _____

    _____

2.  In many states, it is the law for bicycle riders to wear helmets. Should all states have this law? Why or why not?

    _____

    _____

    _____

    _____

3.  The diagram shows bicycle safety rules. What do you think is the best way to inform bicycle riders about these rules?

    _____

    _____

    _____

    _____

# Discussion

Your teacher will split you into small groups. Discuss your responses to Numbers 1 through 3. Take turns sharing your responses and listening to the responses of others. Remember that each group member should stick to the task of his or her role.

When you are finished with your discussion, answer the questions below as a group. Choose one group member to present your group's responses to the class.

# Summary

4. **Did everyone in your group share the same opinion about whether all states should make wearing a bike helmet a law? Explain.**

_____

_____

_____

_____

5. **What were the best reasons given for each side of the argument?**

_____

_____

_____

_____

CCSs: SL.3.4, SL.3.5, SL.3.6

# Lesson 24: Speaking Loudly and Clearly

Have you ever watched someone give a speech? Most likely, you've watched and listened to your principal talk during a school assembly. Or perhaps you've listened to a guest firefighter or police officer talk to your class about a topic.

You may have noticed that these people spoke so that you could hear and understand what they were saying. You may also have a chance to speak to a group of people. You might speak about a book, present a science report, or give a speech if you run for class president. Whatever the task, you will want to speak loud enough for people to hear you and clear enough so people understand what you are saying.

 **TIP 1:  Research your topic.**

When you speak about a topic, you want to give interesting and accurate facts and descriptive details. In Lesson 13, you learned about research. Remember, **research** is the act of finding the information you need to use. You can research using encyclopedias, dictionaries, atlases, newspapers, your own experiences, and other sources. When preparing to give a speech, you will want to research information. Ask yourself these questions to help guide your research:

- What is my topic?

- What is my purpose for speaking? (To tell a funny story, to tell information, to share an opinion, or something else?)

- What are the main points I want to present about my topic?

Use your answers to these questions to help you research.

 **TIP 2:  Take notes and organize your ideas.**

As you research, take notes. Remember from Lesson 22 that **notes** are short phrases and sentences that help remind you of the most important ideas, details, facts, and information you want to share. When you speak about your topic, you will want to present the best examples and details to your audience. Sometimes you might even want to tell your audience where you got your information.

So, when you take notes, be sure to:

- write the source.

- write the author of the source, if this information is given.

### TIP 3: Use descriptive language and interesting facts.

When speaking, you want to be sure that what you say is interesting to your listeners. A good way to do this is to include descriptive details and interesting facts. Descriptive details will help listeners imagine what you are speaking about. Remember, from Lesson 7, sensory words are exciting. So, use sensory words that describe your senses of sight, hearing, touch, taste, and smell. Interesting details and facts will grab the attention of your audience.

### TIP 4: Use proper language when speaking.

In Unit 3, you learned about how to write using proper language. Be sure to also follow these tips when giving a speech.

When you give a speech:

- use complete sentences (with a subject and a verb).
- be sure that your subjects and verbs match.
- use the correct verb tense.
- use adverbs to describe actions and adjectives to describe nouns.
- make your nouns and pronouns match.
- begin your sentences in different ways.
- use simple, compound, and complex sentences.

### TIP 5: Use posters to show your ideas.

Sometimes your teacher might ask you to create a poster to show the ideas in your speech. Posters can help you clearly express your ideas or certain facts and make your presentation more interesting.

You can show your ideas in different ways on a poster. You can paste pictures or images cut from magazines. You can also draw a table, chart, graph, or diagram.

### TIP 6: Speak slowly and clearly.

You learned in Lesson 3 that it is important to read aloud at a good rate and volume. The same is true when you speak aloud. Be sure to speak clearly and at a slow rate so that your listeners can understand you.

### Lesson Practice begins on the following page.

**Directions:** Read the following article about blue whales. Then you will plan a speech about the article.

# Blue Whales

What are the biggest animals that ever lived? Are they elephants? Elephants are pretty big, but they're not the biggest animals ever. Could they be giant dinosaurs? Those animals lived millions of years ago, and they were bigger than elephants are today. But dinosaurs weren't the biggest animals, either.

Here are some hints: The biggest animals do not live on land as elephants do. They have not died out as dinosaurs have. These animals live in the sea, and some of them are living today. Have you guessed the answer yet? Blue whales are the biggest animals that have ever lived on Earth.

All whales are big next to people, but blue whales are huge. A full-grown blue whale can be as long as three school buses parked end to end. And it can weigh as much as 30 elephants put together! Just the heart of a blue whale is as big as a small car. A blue whale can hold enough air in its lungs to stay underwater for almost an hour.

You might think that such a huge animal would be scary and dangerous. But blue whales are very gentle. Have you ever heard people say they are afraid of being swallowed by a whale? They shouldn't be. Although a blue whale's body is huge, it can't swallow anything as big as a person. In fact, blue whales eat tiny shrimp-like animals called *krill*. Krill are from one-half to six inches long.

How can such huge animals stay alive if they eat only tiny sea animals? The answer is that they eat a lot! An adult blue whale eats the weight of a small pickup truck in krill every day.

You might not think whales are much like people. After all, blue whales are huge, and you are not. Blue whales live in the sea, and you live on land. But like people, whales are mammals. Whales have hair on their bodies, though not a lot of it. Their babies are born alive as you were born—not hatched from eggs like fish. Baby whales are called calves. Mother whales feed their babies milk from their bodies, just as human mothers can. And all whales breathe air, just as you breathe air. Whales don't breathe through their mouths, though. They breathe through blowholes on the top of their heads. Some whales have one blowhole. Others have two.

Because blue whales are so big, they don't have any enemies, except for people. Until the 1960s, people hunted and killed whales for the oil in their bodies. Until not long ago, people also hunted whales for food. Some are trying to save them, but blue whales are still in danger. They sometimes get caught in fishing nets. Others get sick from poisoned water. Still others are hunted even though it is against the law. So many blue whales have been killed that scientists worry. They are afraid all blue whales will soon be gone from our planet. If that happens, no one will ever get another chance to see the biggest animal that ever lived.

# Speaking

Plan a speech that explains what should be done to help save blue whales.

**Directions:** Write notes for your speech in the space below.

_____

_____

_____

_____

_____

_____

_____

_____

_____

_____

_____

_____

_____

_____

Using your notes on the previous page, you will present your speech to your class. Your teacher will give you tips for your presentation.

## Speaker's Checklist

✓ **A good presenter:**

☐ uses descriptive language and interesting facts.

☐ uses proper language conventions.

☐ speaks slowly and clearly.

☐ makes a poster when helpful.

# Mechanics Toolbox

### Subject-Verb Agreement

The **subject** tells who or what a sentence is about. The **verb** tells what the subject does. Some subjects are singular. Other subjects are plural.

> Examples:
> The sun shines.
> The dogs bark.

*The sun* is a singular subject. There is just one sun. *The dogs* is a plural subject. There is more than one dog. The verbs *shines* and *bark* tell what each subject does.

A subject and verb need to match in number, or **agree**.

> Examples:
> Franklin runs up the hill. (correct)
> The little boy run to catch up with his big sister. (incorrect)

The plural verb, *run*, does not agree with the singular subject, *The little boy*. The correct sentence is:

> The little boy runs to catch up with his big sister.

### Pronoun-Antecedent Agreement

A **pronoun** is a word that takes the place of a noun. An **antecedent** is the word that a pronoun replaces.

> Example:
> The ducklings followed their mother in a line along the shore. Then they plopped into the lake after her.

In the second sentence, the words *they* and *her* are pronouns. The antecedent of *they* is the plural noun *ducklings*. The antecedent of *her* is the singular noun *mother*.

Pronouns and antecedents need to agree. If the antecedent is more than one, the pronoun needs to show more than one. If the antecedent is male, female, or neither, the pronoun also needs to be male, female, or neither.

> Examples:
> Geoff read another chapter of the mystery before he went to bed. (correct)
> Jessica and Stacey walked to the park. She had a picnic there. (incorrect)

The singular pronoun, *She,* does not agree with the antecedent. *Jessica and Stacey* is more than one. It needs a plural pronoun. The correct sentence is:

> Jessica and Stacey walked to the park. They had a picnic there.

**271**

### Words for Effect

Good writing uses vivid words. Compare these examples:

> The girls <u>went happily</u> across the lawn. (weak word choices)

> The girls <u>skipped</u> and <u>giggled</u> across the lawn. (strong word choices)

The words *skipped* and *giggled* are strong and vivid. They help the reader "see" the girls.

Using more words is not always better. Vivid words can say a lot on their own. Compare these examples:

> The crowd <u>made a lot of noise</u>. (weak word choices)

> The crowd <u>roared</u>. (strong word choice)

### Adjectives and Adverbs

An **adjective** tells more about a noun. The underlined words in these sentences are adjectives:

> Jasmine's bicycle is <u>blue</u>.

> Artie ate his <u>favorite</u> meal of spaghetti and meatballs.

The adjective *blue* tells more about the noun *bicycle*. It tells about the color of the bicycle. The adjective *favorite* tells more about the noun *meal*. It tells that the meal is the one Artie likes best.

An **adverb** tells more about a verb, adjective, or another adverb. It answers the question *How?* The underlined words in these sentences are adverbs:

> The cat slinked <u>quietly</u> out of the room.

> We were happy to go swimming on that <u>very</u> hot Saturday.

The adverb *quietly* tells how the cat slinked. The adverb *very* tells how hot Saturday was.

**Complete Sentences**

A sentence tells a complete thought. It has a subject and a verb.

Example:
We laughed.

This sentence is short, but it is complete. It has a subject, *We*. The verb, *laughed*, tells what the subject does.

Some sentences tell two or more complete thoughts. Words like *and*, *but*, and *or* are used to connect the thoughts. In the following sentence, the complete thoughts are underlined.

Dark clouds covered the sky and rain began to fall.

In other sentences, a less important idea is added to a complete thought. Words like *when*, *because*, *if*, and *after* are used to connect the less important idea to the main thought. In the following sentences, the less important idea is underlined once and the main thought is underlined twice.

My father wakes up when the birds begin to sing.

Because he leaves for work so early, my father also comes home early.

A **run-on sentence** tells two or more thoughts without using any connecting words.

Example:
The sirens grew louder and louder, the fire trucks rushed down the avenue.

You can correct a run-on sentence by splitting it into two complete sentences. You can also correct it by adding a connecting word.

Examples:
The sirens grew louder and louder. The fire trucks rushed down the avenue.
The sirens grew louder and louder, <u>and</u> the fire trucks rushed down the avenue.

A **sentence fragment** does not tell a complete thought.

Example:
The panda that was just born at the zoo.

The subject, *The panda*, does not have a verb. You can correct a sentence fragment by completing the thought. The fragment is completed by adding a verb.

Example:
The panda that was just born at the zoo <u>is</u> still too young for visitors to see.

**Mechanics Toolbox**

## Confused Words

**Homophones** are two or more words that sound alike but are spelled differently and mean different things. They are easy to confuse. Here are some homophones.

| Homophones and Meanings | Examples |
| --- | --- |
| **A lot:** many | Janice used <u>a lot</u> of fruit to make a big salad for the party. |
| **Allot:** to give out | We will <u>allot</u> five cards to each player. |
| **Board:** a plank | We need just one more <u>board</u> to complete our tree house. |
| **Bored:** uninterested, dull | On the second day of the car trip, Terrence was <u>bored</u>. |
| **Hear:** to take in sounds | We could <u>hear</u> the children shouting before we saw them. |
| **Here:** at this place | We keep a spare key <u>here</u>, under this rock. |
| **It's:** it is | <u>It's</u> not likely to snow in June. |
| **Its:** belonging to it | The garden is famous for <u>its</u> prize-winning roses. |
| **Knew:** past tense of *know* | Johnny <u>knew</u> the name of every student at his school. |
| **New:** opposite of *old* | Angela wore her <u>new</u> bracelet the day after her birthday. |
| **Their:** belonging to them | <u>Their</u> house has a big porch, whereas ours has none. |
| **There:** at that place | If you go <u>there</u> to visit, they will ask you to stay for lunch. |
| **They're:** they are | <u>They're</u> friendly and enjoy company. |
| **Weak:** opposite of *strong* | The baby birds were still too <u>weak</u> to fly. |
| **Week:** a series of seven days | In one more <u>week</u>, our vacation will begin. |

These commonly confused words sound almost the same but have different meanings. Here are some examples.

| Commonly Confused Words and Meanings | Examples |
|---|---|
| **Accept:** to agree | I hope that you <u>accept</u> our invitation to play in the recital! |
| **Except:** not including | Everyone had fun at the game <u>except</u> for Russell, who was too tired. |
| **Affect:** to cause a change | I cried, but the end of the movie did not <u>affect</u> my mother. |
| **Effect:** result | The floods were not the only <u>effect</u> of the heavy rains. |
| **Close:** to shut | Mrs. Lee asked me to <u>close</u> the door behind me. |
| **Clothes:** garments, such as a shirt or pants | I wore my best <u>clothes</u> to the wedding, including the red tie my grandfather gave me. |
| **Loose:** opposite of *tight* | My shoelaces were <u>loose</u>, and I almost tripped on them. |
| **Lose:** opposite of *win* | It never feels good to <u>lose</u>. |
| **Than:** in comparison with | My sister likes playing soccer much more <u>than</u> I do. |
| **Then:** at that time | We did not know as much <u>then</u> as we do now. |
| **Weather:** the state of the atmosphere in a place | The <u>weather</u> here changes quickly, from sunshine to snow in moments. |
| **Whether:** shows a choice | <u>Whether</u> or not you come with me, I am going swimming. |

The verbs *lie* and *lay* are also commonly confused. Their meanings are similar. Also, the past tense of *lie* is *lay*. However, *lie* never has an object. *Lay* always has an object. Here are some examples.

| | |
|---|---|
| **Lie:** to rest, recline | Go <u>lie</u> on the bed until you feel better. |
| **Lay:** past tense of *lie* | Thomas <u>lay</u> there until dinner was ready. |
| **Lay:** to put down | I <u>lay</u> the flowers on the table. |
| **Laid:** past tense of *lay* | Irma <u>laid</u> the tools she needed on the counter. |

## ▶ <u>Word Choice</u>

Good writing uses exact words. Compare these examples:

> The boy was <u>tired</u>.
> The boy was <u>sleepy</u>.
> The boy was <u>worn out</u>.

*Sleepy* and *tired* have similar meanings. The word *sleepy* gives more information than the word *tired*. It tells the way the boy is tired: he needs sleep. The word *sleepy* is a more exact word than *tired*.

*Worn out* and *tired* also have similar meanings. *Worn out* is also more exact than *tired*. It tells that the boy is tired from playing or working hard.

Like vivid words, exact words can say a lot on their own. Compare these examples:

> The class <u>had a good time</u> at the farm. (weak word choice)
> The class <u>enjoyed</u> the farm. (strong word choice)

Here are some weak words and some stronger words you can use in their place.

| Weak Words | Strong Words |
|---|---|
| **Cold** | • chilly<br>• frozen<br>• wintery |
| **Warm** | • boiling<br>• burning<br>• tropical |
| **Big** | • huge<br>• giant<br>• vast |
| **Small** | • puny<br>• slight<br>• tiny |
| **Happy** | • delighted<br>• pleased<br>• thrilled |
| **Sad** | • depressed<br>• gloomy<br>• miserable |

##  Punctuation

Every sentence ends with a punctuation mark. A sentence that tells a statement ends with a **period (.)**. For example:

> We go to the farmers' market on Saturday mornings.

A sentence that gives a command also ends with a period. For example:

> Please get me a pound of apples when you are there.

A sentence that asks a question ends with a **question mark (?)**. For example:

> Does anyone sell fresh eggs at the market?

A sentence that shows excitement ends with an **exclamation point (!)**. For example:

> That pumpkin weighs 300 pounds!

A **quotation** shows the exact words that someone said. A quotation begins and ends with **quotation marks (" ")**. For example,

> Rami said, "Those cider doughnuts are the best."

Notice that a **comma (,)** is used before the quotation. In the example below, a comma is used at the end of the quotation:

> "I like the doughnuts from our bakery better," Allison said.

If the quotation asks a question, a question mark is used. If the quotation shows excitement, an exclamation point is used.

> Examples:
> "Is the market also open on Wednesdays?" Rami asked.
> "I wish it were open every day!" Allison exclaimed.

# Notes

# Notes

# Notes

# Notes

# Notes

# Notes

# Notes

# Notes

# Notes

# Notes

**Notes**